in books that come with oracle cards. Andrew Anderson shows the power of storytelling in shaping the way we envisage both forces of nature and deities.

Lucya Starza, author of Pagan Portals titles on *Candle Magic, Poppets and Magical Dolls, Guided Visualisations, Scrying,* and *The Wheel of the Year*, and the Gothic novel, *Erosion*

Andrew Anderson takes us on a fascinating literary and cultural journey in search of the elusive roots of *Herne the Hunter*. It is an enlightening and enjoyable read, busting open some myths and shining a light on Herne's surprising evolution and ever-changing face. Andrew illustrates the mystery of how the archetypal can come to inhabit the stories we tell in unexpected ways.

Eimear Burke, Chosen Chief of the Order of Bards, Ovates and Druids

What People Are Saying About

Herne the Hunter

From Star Carr in Yorkshire to Windsor Great Park via the Trois Freres caves, from folk trickster to deity via Shakespeare and Victorian gothic, this is a masterly summation of the origins of a beloved Green God of the twenty-first century. The author reveals Herne's origins and reminds us that ultimately, archetypes can never be confined, but will always exist on their own terms.
Penny Billington, author of *The Path of Druidry, The Wisdom of Birch, Oak and Yew* and *Nine ways to charm a Dryad*

Andrew Anderson is a wordsmith who weaves magic into stories and translates that onto the page. With *Herne the Hunter* he brings together a tale of magic, mystery and perhaps even a little mayhem, with history and lore woven through. Anderson captures the essence of this intriguing figure perfectly. Fact, fiction or a bit of both? If that question interests you, I encourage you to read the book!
Rachel Patterson, Witch and best-selling author of over 30 books on Witchcraft including *Gods & Goddesses of England, The Triple Goddess* and *The Cailleach.*

Andrew Anderson has produced a gem of a book here, tracing the evolution of Herne the hunter from his early Shakespearean roots to a beloved god of modern British paganism. Anderson's scholarship here is excellent - just what we need to uncover the facts for a figure whose roots and branches are as twisted as an old oak. But these facts are in safe hands with Anderson who knows this does nothing to diminish Herne's power - his fondness for the god that drew so many of us towards paganism

in the first place, is tangible and infectious. I always think if we didn't know him by the name Herne, we'd know him by some other name, as we need a god of the forest, and he is the one who came. This is book is essential reading for all those who love him, and fills an important gap on the bookshelf. 5 stars.
Danu Forest (MA Celtic Studies) Traditional Wisewoman, folklorist and Celtic Scholar

Challenging, evocative, ground breaking... Anderson's *Herne the Hunter: The Lord of the Forest,* is an expose on a figure so many believe they know well. Relying on his Shakespearean studies background, Anderson takes readers on the literary journey through the development and apotheosis of a modern English God. From the first mention of Herne in Shakespeare's *The Merry Wives of Windsor,* Anderson masterfully covers, with no stone left unturned, the four-hundred-year odyssey of Herne and his mythos. Highly recommended.
Benjamin Stimpson, author of *Of Doves & Ravens: The Witches and Wisefolk of Wales and the Borders*

Herne – is he a pagan god, the ghost of hanged man, an English folk hero, a spirit of the wildwood, or a character created by Shakespeare to entertain Elizabethan audiences? Andrew Anderson's *Pagan Portals – Herne the Hunter* shows that he has been depicted as all of these. Fascinating and meticulously researched, this book takes a deep dive into the history, legends, myths, and creative interpretations that have turned a horned man said to haunt the woods of Windsor into one of the most popular archetypes honoured in modern paganism. As a student of literature, I was personally fascinated to learn that Herne's metamorphosis is primarily due to the way writers have re-imagined him, from Shakespearean theatre, to Gothic novels, to television's *Robin of Sherwood* and even descriptions

Herne the Hunter

Lord of the Forest

Previous Titles by This Author

The Ritual of Writing
ISBN 978 1 78904 153 8

Artio and Artaois
ISBN 978 1 78904 432 1

The Magic of Cats
ISBN 978 1 80341 066 1

Herne the Hunter

Lord of the Forest

Andrew Anderson

Illustrated by Hannah Willow

MOON BOOKS

London, UK

Washington, DC, USA

CollectiveInk

First published by Moon Books, 2026
Moon Books is an imprint of Collective Ink Ltd.,
Unit 11, Shepperton House, 89 Shepperton Road, London, N1 3DF
office@collectiveinkbooks.com
www.collectiveinkbooks.com
www.moon-books.net

For distributor details and how to order please visit the 'Ordering' section on our website.

ISBN: 978 1 80341 527 7
978 1 917991 36 0 (ebook)
Library of Congress Control Number: 2025943379

A CIP catalogue record for this book is available from the British Library.

Design: Lapiz Digital Services

UK: Printed and bound by CPI Group (UK) Ltd, Croydon, CR0 4YY
US: Printed and bound by Thomson-Shore, 7300 West Joy Road, Dexter, MI 48130

The manufacturer's authorised representative in the EU for product safety is:
eucomply OÜ - Pärnu mnt 139b-14, 11317 Tallinn, Estonia,
hello@ eucompliancepartner.com, www.eucompliancepartner.com

Contents

For my brother, Jeffrey, who fostered my love of
Herne the Hunter by introducing me to *Robin of Sherwood*.

And for my sister, Lesley, who took me out
on Saturday nights so I had to record it.

Acknowledgements

An enormous thank you to Hannah for offering to illustrate another of my books. It is always such a thrill to see your magical artwork connected with my words. I can never thank you enough for your ongoing generosity.

Thank you to Trevor, Matty, Rachel and all at Moon Books for their support and patience in waiting for this manuscript.

Thank you to Becky for your help with everything, from those initial discussions to the final proof-reading edits.

And to Emma, because she always checks to see if I have mentioned her and it's about time I did.

Introduction

Who Is Herne?

Exercise: Meeting Herne the Hunter

Before you begin reading this book, I would like you to take an inner journey to meet Herne the Hunter as you know him. Set aside plenty of time for this journey, when you have no other pressures or demands on your time.

Sit or lay somewhere you are comfortable and imagine you are walking through one of England's beautiful oak forests. It is summer time. The light around you is dappled by the leaves of the trees above you. The landscape around you buzzes and hums with life. Take time to notice the details, the trees, the shafts of light, the insects.

You find yourself entering a clearing, a grove within the forest. On one side of the clearing is an enormous oak tree, far bigger than any of the others you have found so far. Take a seat in front of the oak, at a respectful distance away from it. And wait.

When you are ready, and when he is ready, Herne the Hunter will step out from the trunk of the oak tree and stand before you. What does he look like? What is he wearing? Does he have antlers on an otherwise human head or is his whole head that of a deer? Is he carrying or holding anything?

Spend time in the grove just being with Herne. You do not have to do anything. Neither does he. Just be there in that woodland space with him. If he does do anything or speak to you, remember what he says.

And when the time is right, when you feel ready and when Herne is ready too, thank him for his presence. He will step back into his oak. You will find your way out of the grove and walk back through the abundant forest, back to your physical body and current surroundings. Emerge back into this world gently. And when you are fully returned, make some notes about your experiences, writing down as much about

Herne as you can remember. It is important that we acknowledge Herne as he is to us at this point of our journey because that view of him may be about to change.

In early 2023, the UK television station Channel 4 showed a wonderful short series called *Grayson Perry's Full English*. Perry is an extraordinary artist and social commentator who began by asking the central question 'who are the English' against the backdrop of a turbulent few years for the nation: "Now we're out of Europe," Perry mused, "with a new monarch on the throne and the growing possibility that the days of the United Kingdom may be numbered." He clearly felt it was time to interrogate English national identity.

In the first episode, Perry journeys around the south of England, visiting individuals and communities to discuss their view of Englishness. At the same time, he collects an item from each of them which represents their vision of England. Later in the programme, he meets with a couple named only as Nick and Nadia. They organise trespass events on the estates of England's major landowners. Their actions are motivated by the belief that the "English don't have access to England" and have not for centuries, due to historic land enclosure. Nick, who we will find out more about in Chapter 5, states that the English only have access to 8% of their countryside and 3% of rivers, raising the question "Is England crowded or is it crowded because we occupy the corridors in between these vast mansion estates of empty space?" By way of protest, Nick and others walk onto land to which access is restricted or forbidden. Such a trespass event at Englefield Estate near Reading is shown in all its riotously peaceful vibrancy. A large crowd, dressed colourfully in "neon Pagan" costumes of different folkloric characters, walk and dance their way to an oak tree at the heart of the estate, where they sing songs and discuss the land with each other.

During the trespass, Nick is seen putting on his folklore inspired outfit. He has a stag's skull, complete with antlers, which is encased in gold. It sits on his hat but can be pulled down to cover his face. This is the object which he picks to become part of Perry's collection representing Englishness. "It's Herne the Hunter," Nick explains, "He's a local deity." Here, Nick is recalling the tale of Herne as a one-time resident of Windsor Great Park, which is only about twenty miles from Reading. Nick warmly utters "Good old Herne," showing a real affection for him. As he hands the skull over, he warns Perry "I wouldn't put it on. Some shit happens," as if this mask, which we later find out was made in 2021, channels an ancient wild and elemental force of which we need to be wary.

Being a child of the late twentieth century, I grew up with such images of the ancient and primal Herne all around me, notably in books such as *The Dark is Rising* by Susan Cooper, John Masefield's novel *The Box of Delights* and its 1984 television adaptation, and the contemporary television series *Robin of Sherwood*. The last few years have seen a profusion of representations of Herne, such as Zoe Gilbert's brilliant 2022 novel *Mischief Acts*. Around the same time as I watched Perry's programme, I bought myself some beautiful Herne the Hunter prayer beads from a craftsperson called Celtic Spirit Charms. And Mark Ryan and John Matthew's beautiful card set, *The Sherwood Oracle*, published in 2024, includes a card of Herne, with the book stating that: "Though he may seem to belong to other and later traditions, Herne is part of the lore of the wildwood."[1]

However, we cannot trace the recorded lineage of Herne the Hunter back very far at all. The first written record of him is found in 1602, just 400 years ago. Rachel Patterson's 2023 book, *The Gods and Goddesses of England*, contains a good-sized section on Herne, which begins with a rather mysterious turn of phrase: "Herne has an unusual story that puts him in the realm of the gods. There is no physical evidence he was worshipped as such."[2] Ronald Hutton goes one step further in his seminal text, *Pagan Britain*, stating that "Herne's status as a pagan god, at any rate, is very doubtful."[3]

This book will stick closely to the figure of Herne himself. It will not be a consideration of horned gods or such topics as the use of antlers in shamanic or ritual practice, focusing instead on how Herne came to be seen in the context of these ideas and practises. In recent years, Herne has appeared in numerous guises, meaning that this cannot be an exhaustive study of every text where Herne is mentioned. I will not, for example, be considering Terry Pratchett's inspired parody, Herne the Hunted, the god of hunted animals. Instead, I will focus on five key texts across five centuries to examine the different perspectives they give us of Herne the Hunter. By taking a chronological approach, we will be able to see the process by which Herne came to be considered a deity in the popular imagination, when he started as little more than a theatrical joke. Each text gives us a version of Herne that is unique yet interconnected, and their creators have different cultural reasons for presenting him as they have. As such, we will need to consider the wider context of each text and how Herne was seen in some other works of the time. Together, these five texts both create and reflect the image of Herne the Hunter who lives in our collective understanding, whether we are aware of them or not.

There is a deep and widespread affection for Herne amongst practicing Pagans. That phrase of Nick's, "Good old Herne," is one I have heard a number of times while writing this book. Our feelings about Herne are sometimes at odds with what our ancestors wrote down about him. Even when they did record him in their works, he was often the subject of works of fiction, both dramatic and literary, where he was used by a plot device rather than being honoured as a figure in his own right. He was used to conjure terror and belly laughs, not devotion. Even the texts which attempt a more distanced, factual evaluation of him and his story are often weighed down with difficult contextual issues or mired in contradiction and confusion. It is not until the nineteenth century that anyone proposes an association between Herne and deity, by which stage it is more of a leap of faith than anything that can be proven.

So, just how ancient is the figure of Herne the Hunter and where should we start searching for him? Do we begin by plunging into the wildwoods of Sherwood or exploring under the oak trees of Windsor Great Park? The answer is neither.

We begin this journey in the Forest of Arden...

Chapter 1

Shakespeare's Device

"Great ragg'd horns" by Hannah Willow

The first time the name of Herne the Hunter appears in print is in the 1602 quarto edition of William Shakespeare's play *The Merry Wives of Windsor*. Although the play did not appear in print until the early 1600s, it is believed to have been written some years earlier, probably around 1597. The play involves one of Shakespeare's most beloved characters, Sir John Falstaff, attempting to seduce the wives of two of Windsor's most prominent citizens. As the play draws towards its close, the wives, Mistress Page and Mistress Ford, irritated by his unwelcome attention, decide to play trick on Falstaff persuading him to get dressed up as Herne the Hunter.

It is in Act 4, scene 4, when they are devising their plot, that the Merry Wives and their husbands first mention Herne (25-40):

Mistress Page
There is an old tale goes that Herne the Hunter,
Sometimes keeper here in Windsor Forest,
Doth all the winter-time, at still midnight,
Walk round about an oak, with great ragg'd horns;
And there he blasts the trees, and takes the cattle,
And makes the milch-kine yield blood, and shakes a chain
In a most hideous and dreadful manner.
You have heard of such a spirit, and well you know
The superstitious idle-headed eld
Received and did deliver to our age
This tale of Herne the Hunter for a truth.

Page
Why, yet there want not many that do fear
In deep of night to walk by this Herne's Oak.
But what of this?

Mistress Ford
Marry, this is our device:
That Falstaff at that oak shall meet with us,
Disguised like Herne, with huge horns on his head.[1]

Mistress Page develops the plan by arranging for a number of small children, dressed up "like urchins, oafs, and fairies, green and white, / With rounds of waxen tapers on their heads, / And rattles in their hands" (47-49) to jump out on the unsuspecting Falstaff and scare him into telling the truth about his seduction, therefore embarrassing him in front of the whole community.

Before we get into a consideration of Herne's presentation in the play, I want to take a very quick detour. Most of this book will revolve around the importance of evidence, considering what documents and study of historical context tells us about Herne, trying to unpick where our beliefs about him came from. So, before we look at the text of *Merry Wives* more closely, I want to briefly deal with the speculation around the authorship of the play. In other words, who wrote Shakespeare? This may seem like an odd detour to take, but, as you will see over the first chapters of this book, Shakespeare is almost as important to Herne's story as Herne himself. There are also some striking similarities between the way we have treated Shakespeare and Herne, which will become clear as this chapter progresses.

Perhaps the best resource about the authorship of Shakespeare's plays is James Shapiro's book *Contested Will: Who Wrote Shakespeare?* (2010) Shapiro not only examines the evidence around several of the figures who have been proposed as the real author of the plays and poems of Shakespeare but, perhaps more importantly, considers why this question ever arose and why many people still question the authorship today. "While Shakespeare was a product of an early modern world" Shapiro writes, "the controversy over his authorship of his works is the creation of a modern one."[2] His argument is that William Shakespeare, man of Stratford, does not fit with our modern sense of what a writer should be. The first stirrings of the authorship question did not begin until 1785, over 150 years after Shakespeare died. At that point, a Stratford local named James Wilmot began searching for Shakespeare's papers, such as his diaries, notebooks, and journals. After all, as a writer, Shakespeare must have left behind lots of documentary evidence of his writing process, right? Well, no, not necessarily. As Shapiro points out, "Shakespeare did not live, as we do, in an age of memoir. Few at the time kept personal diaries or wrote personal essays."[3] A cache of Shakespeare's personal papers and, perhaps even more excitingly, a new play called *Vortigern* did appear in the 1790s but they turned out to be fake. They had been forged by William Henry Ireland, much to the shame and embarrassment of his father, Samuel Ireland, a notable admirer of Shakespeare, who had published a folio of the documents, believing them to be genuine.

It is this pursuit of evidence about Shakespeare's personality, our need to know the person behind the plays, which began the authorship question back in the 1780s and which still drives it today. The advocates for the other proposed candidates take the lack of personal information about the man of Stratford and fill it with assumptions, hearsay, and coincidences about alternative authors, bringing a sense of personality to the mysterious genius who hides behind the words. "Much of what has been written about the authorship of Shakespeare's plays follows the contours of a detective story," Shapiro writes, "which is not at all surprising, since the authorship question and the 'whodunnit' emerged at the same historical moment."[4] In much the same way as we are compelled to understand the motivation of the murderer in a whodunnit, we have the same drive to understand the personality of the figure many consider to be the greatest writer of all time. Surely a man from a small town in Warwickshire, the son of a mere glovemaker, could not possibly have written such a diverse range of plays and poems. It must have been someone far more educated, connected, and charismatic, like Christopher Marlowe, the Earl of Oxford or Francis Bacon, right?

Well, no. While the advocates for alternative authors can weave you a tantalising web of questions and possibilities, what they cannot do is provide you with any actual documentary evidence of their claims. And while we may not have much evidence about the man of Stratford's personality, there is an enormous amount of evidence that William Shakespeare, the boy who grew up in the house on Henley Street in Stratford-upon-Avon, was the man who wrote the plays and poems attributed to him. Yes, there are a few gaps in the timeline but you would expect that for a life lived over 400 years ago. The same could be said for many of his contemporaries and yet no questions about the authorship of their work are ever raised. That is not to say Shakespeare wrote every word. Much academic work of the past 20 years has explored the possibility of Shakespeare writing collaboratively with other writers. Books such as Darren Freebury-Jones's *Shakespeare's Borrowed Feathers* show Shakespeare as a writer directly influenced by and working with others. As such, academic approaches now interrogate Shakespeare as a collaborative artist rather than searching for an alternative candidate for his authorship.

While many of the conspiracy theories around the authorship of Shakespeare's work involve great stretches of the imagination, Shapiro notes that it is that very sense of imagination which such theories attack. "What I feel most disheartening about the claims that Shakespeare of Stratford lacked the life experience to have written the plays is that it diminishes the very thing that makes him so exceptional: his imagination. As an aspiring actor, Shakespeare must have displayed a talent for imagining himself as any number of characters onstage. When he turned to writing, he demonstrated an even more powerful imaginative capacity, one that allowed him to create roles of such depth and complexity ... that even the least of them, four centuries later, seems fully human and distinctive."[5] What is interesting to consider here is that one of Shakespeare's greatest imaginative creations could have been a relatively minor character, a ghost from one of his comedies who, four centuries later, is now considered to be a god.

So, did Shakespeare just make up Herne the Hunter as a theatrical device, as a way of conveniently finishing his play, or did he use an existing piece of folklore from Windsor? There are hints within the text itself that Shakespeare could be referencing some kind of oral tradition which comes from the area. Mistress Page says it is an "old tale" (4.4.25) which "The superstitious idle-headed eld / Received and did deliver to our age" (4.4.33-34). In other words, this is a story which the older generation have passed down to the characters in the play, probably verbally. Of course, the issue with stories being passed down through an oral tradition is that there are, obviously, no written record of them, so it becomes impossible to trace them back further. But it is possible that Shakespeare could have heard such a piece of folklore while passing through the area.

1597, the year that we believe *The Merry Wives of Windsor* was written, was an important year for William Shakespeare as he bought the largest private house in Stratford-upon-Avon, known as New Place. His son, Hamnet, had died in 1596 and we believe that Shakespeare began travelling back to Stratford from London more regularly after this tragedy, to live with his wife and two daughters in their large home. While we cannot be exactly sure of the route he would have taken to London, work has been done to recreate one possible route "using existing footpaths, bridleways and a few minor roads"[6]. This is called Shakespeare's Way and is a 146-mile path connecting Shakespeare's Birthplace in Stratford-upon-Avon with the reconstructed Globe Theatre on the south bank of the Thames in London. The route runs to the north of Windsor, so it is possible that Shakespeare could have heard the story of Herne on his way to and from London. While there is no evidence that Shakespeare or his acting company ever performed in Windsor, references within the play to The Garter Inn, a real venue in the town, suggest that he had visited it and was familiar with the place where he set his play. Similarly, references in the play to a particular oak tree which is haunted by Herne suggests that Shakespeare may have been using a specific piece of folklore tied to a specific place.

So, what do scholars and researchers make of the idea that Shakespeare was using a real piece of folklore in his play? Well, frankly, not much. "The story of Herne the Hunter and his oak is not genuine folklore" states Leo Salingar, "but Shakespeare's invention."[7] Giorgio Melchiori notes that "The tale or legend seems to be of Shakespeare's own invention"[8] while T.W. Craik also posits that Herne is "Known only in this play, and so [is] probably Shakespeare's invention."[9] Jeremy Harte, whose 1996 article *Herne the Hunter – A Case of Mistaken Identity* was the first to pull together a historical account of the creation and development of Herne's role in modern paganism, is far more direct in his evaluation. "Herne is a character. He has meant many different things in many different performances ... I can find no evidence of a pre-1597 performance in which he played the part of a god."[10] Harte's argument is that Herne is purely a theatrical device and that "...the final scene of the *Merry Wives* is too carefully crafted in its dramatic effect to be a mere report of local folklore." Delving deep into the theatricality of the final scene, Harte is adamant that "Literal transcriptions of folk belief were not [Shakespeare's] line."[11]

So, if the figure of Herne presented in *The Merry Wives of Windsor* is not reflective of a piece of folklore, what dramatic function does Herne have within the play and how does this help our understanding of him? Well, perhaps the first thing to note is that Herne is referred to by Mistress Page as a "spirit," the ghost of a human keeper who terrorises the local community, rather than a deity. However, just because a play written in the 1590s presented him as a scary ghost does not mean that the figure of Herne had always had such spooky connotations. In fact, many pre-Christian deities had been turned into such figures of local folklore:

> Of all the channels through which pagan ideas and images flowed into Christian culture, by far the most

> important and effective consisted of the literature, art and orally transmitted stories which depicted the nature and seeds of deities ... By such means, pagan goddesses and gods who, in strict early theology, had to be regarded as demons came to be treated with affection and admiration by many Christians of differing denominations and degrees of piety; even though they were religiously neutered by being seen as figures of allegory or fiction.[12]

So, it is possible that the "old tale" Shakespeare references at the start of Mistress Page's speech may be harking back to an ancient time when Herne was considered as a deity rather than a "spirit." However, this is where it gets difficult to unpick the difference between any authentic oral tradition surrounding Herne and the way he is presented in the play, because the figure that we find in *The Merry Wives of Windsor* shares many similarities with ghosts and spirits in other theatrical and literary works.

To recap, Mistress Page says that Herne the Hunter:

> Doth all the winter-time, at still midnight,
> Walk round about an oak, with great ragg'd horns;
> And there he blasts the trees, and takes the cattle,
> And makes the milch-kine yield blood, and shakes a chain
> In a most hideous and dreadful manner. (4:4:27-31)

The first thing to note here is the time that Herne appears: Midnight. That is the same time that the most famous ghost in Shakespeare's works, the Ghost of Hamlet's Father, appears. In act 1, scene 1 of *Hamlet*, Barnardo notes that "'Tis now struck twelve" (5) just before the Ghost appears on stage for the first time, while, later in the same scene, Marcellus states that "Thus twice before, and just at this dead hour," (64) he has seen the ghost. The Ghost's final scripted appearance comes shortly after Hamlet's announces "'Tis now the very witching time of night, / When churchyards yawn and hell itself breathes out / Contagion to this world." (3.2.377-379.) So, like Hamlet's father, Herne's ghost only appears at midnight, a time which, paraphrasing Hamlet's speech, is known to some as 'The Witching Hour'[13]. This marks him out as a spirit of potentially evil intent although, as the Ghost of Hamlet's Father shows us, this is not always the case.

Mistress Page reports that Herne "shakes a chain / In a most hideous and dreadful manner" (4.4.30-31). Later, in Act 5, scene 1, Mistress Quickly tells Falstaff: "I'll provide you a chain, and I'll do what I can to get you a pair of horns" (5-6). While the pair of horns have become central to the imagery of Herne (more on this below), within the folklore of the play, the chain seems an equally significant identifying prop, although, as Craik points out "No dramatic use is made of the chain, nor is it referred to in 5.5, and it is hardly ever carried on by Falstaff in performance."[14] Ghosts rattling chains have become a frequent folkloric, theatrical and literary device, the most famous example being the chains carried Jacob Marley in Charles Dickens' 1893 novella *A Christmas Carol*. However, the earliest recorded case of a ghost in chains dates to the writings of Pliny the Younger in Rome: "In the dead of the night a noise, resembling the clashing of iron, was frequently heard, which, if you listened more attentively, sounded like the rattling of chains..."[15] The association of Herne with both midnight and chains are dramatically significant because they communicate clearly to the audience that he is a ghost.

In the speech by Mistress Page, Shakespeare frames Herne the Hunter as a trickster. His focus on "blasting trees," stealing and tormenting cattle and, therefore, their owners, calls to mind another "shrewd and knavish sprite" in Shakespeare's work, Robin Goodfellow, or Puck, from *A Midsummer Night's Dream*.

In Act 2, scene 1, the Fairy asks Puck if they are indeed the notorious figure who:

> … frights the maidens of the villag'ry,
> Skim milk, and sometimes labour in the quern,
> And bootless make the breathless housewife churn,
> And sometime make the drink to bear no balm –
> Mislead night wanderers, laughing at their harm? (1.2.35-39)

There is definitely a connection between the reported actions of these two figures, even if Puck appears rather cheekier and Herne scarier (although the way that the inhabitants of Windsor go sneaking around his tree at midnight means he cannot be that frightening!). While we may feel that this connection between these two notable figures of English folklore shows that Shakespeare worked elements of actual, established folklore into his plays, Salingar points out that these "trickeries ascribed to Puck in *A Midsummer Night's Dream*"[16] have no grounding in folklore of the time. In other words, Shakespeare made them up.

So, if the time Herne appears, his chain and antics are likely to be theatrical inventions of Shakespeare, what is left that could, possibly, relate to an oral piece of folklore?

His horns.

And while Herne's horns have become the thing which have defined him in subsequent centuries, they are the most theatrically important feature he has. Herne must have horns for the action of the play to unfold as it does.

Back in 1597, when the play was written, the image of a man with horns on his head was used to symbolise a cuckold, or a man whose wife was sleeping with other men. Shakespeare uses the image repeatedly in his works, such as *Much Ado about Nothing*, where Benedict says "…pluck off the bull's horns and set them in my forehead" (1.1.246-247), *As You Like it,* where Touchstone declares "many a man has good horns, and knows no end of them" (3.3.48-49), and *Titus Andronicus,* where characters joke that Tamora's adultery may make her husband's hunting hounds mistake "him for a stag." (2.3.71) The image is a complex one and relates to the etymology of the word, cuckold, which derives from Old French word Cocu, or Cuckoo.[17] Cuckoo chicks grow up in other birds' nests and, to observers, are obviously not the chick of the bird which is feeding it. However, the birds carry on feeding the chick, seemingly oblivious to the fact they are raising the young of another. In much the same way, the horns on the head of the cuckold are obvious to everyone else, but cannot be seen by the man whose wife is having an affair. Every time he looks up, the horns disappear, meaning he cannot work out why everyone is laughing at him. In *Merry Wives,* Shakespeare adapts this image slightly and puts the horns on the head of the cuckolder, Falstaff, rather than on the husbands of Mistresses Page and Ford; after all, the wives remain completely loyal to their husbands during the play.

Herne's horns are so important to the plot that they even constituted his original name. Here I need to amend the opening line of this chapter where I claimed that "The first time the name Herne the Hunter appears in print is in the 1602 quarto edition of William Shakespeare's play *The Merry Wives of Windsor*." In fact, in the quarto edition of the play, which was reprinted in 1619, the character is named not as Herne but as Horne the Hunter; the spelling was not changed to more familiar Herne until the first folio, which was printed in 1623. In fact, the whole account of 'Horne' is different in the quarto, with Mistress Page stating:

> Oft haue you heard since *Horne* the hunter dyed,
> That women to affright their little children,
> Ses that he walks in shape of a great stagge.

The quarto edition is "agreed to be based on a stage version"[18], possibly one remembered by a member of the cast, so the use of Horne as a name for the character, while interesting and with historic precedence, as we will see in Chapter 3, is not entirely reliable. As such, most editors default to the spelling found in the folio, which is felt to be more authoritative (a notable exception being Walter Wilson Greg, an influential twentieth-century bibliographer, who believed that the spelling should remain as Horne). It is interesting to note that the variant spelling remained unchallenged in print for over twenty years before it was changed. The naming of the character as Horne helps us cut through the mythology which has grown around him and get straight to his dramatic purpose as marking out Falstaff as a cuckolder and a 'horny' old man. Melchiori believes that the name Horne is "somewhat too obviously allusive" to these qualities and that changing the name to Herne was more subtle, suggesting "the heron, a water bird that could be found on the Thames banks."[19] There is some evidence to suggest that Herne, as a surname, derives from word Heron.

It is worth dwelling, albeit briefly, on Herne's full title here and a possible perceived contradiction between his role as a hunter and his mortal job as a keeper. The Online OED has several definitions of the word keeper, but in the context of forestry the term means "An officer who has the charge of a forest, woods, or grounds."[20] In Herne's case, he is likely meant to be a keeper of the deer in Windsor Great Park and would, therefore, be a keeper for the monarch. Does this not sit at odds with his name, 'the Hunter'? Not necessarily. Later in the play, Falstaff also refers to his disguise as a "woodman" (5.5.26), which the OED describes as "One who hunts game in a wood or forest; a huntsman."[21] There does seem to be a correlation between looking after the game and being involved in hunting it, with permission, of course. The term 'woodman' also has sexual connotations, as we shall see later in this chapter, so it is possible that the term 'Hunter' has those connotations too.

So, what would Falstaff's disguise have looked like on stage at the time the play was written? Here there is some disagreement between Shakespeareans, and between the quarto and folio texts. The quarto contains a stage direction which reads *"Enter sir Iohn* [Falstaff] *with a Bucks head vpon him."* This, twinned with a later reference from the character, Evans, that he has "His bodie man, his head a buck" could imply that Falstaff is not only wearing antlers but has his whole face covered by a stag's head. While this may seem rather elaborate, there is precedence in Shakespeare's work for such a transformation. In *A Midsummer Night's Dream,* likely written in 1594 or 1595, The character of Bottom is transformed by Robin Goodfellow, appearing on stage with an ass's head. The performance company clearly has the prop of an ass's head to achieve this transformation, so it is possible that it was adapted, with the addition of antlers, for *Merry Wives*. This kind of costume would also heighten the comedy of the scene and add to the knock-about humour of the finale. There are also some textual echoes of this within the play, where Bottom's line "This is to make an ass of me" (3.1.114) is echoed in Falstaff's lament "I do begin to perceive that I am made an ass" (5.5.118).

Of course, it is by no means certain that a full stag's head was used; after all, Mistress Quickly simply says she will "get [Falstaff] a pair of horns" (5.3.6). Again, we know from other plays at the time that theatrical companies had such props. For example, in Marlowe's *Tragical History of Doctor Faustus,* a Knight who mocks Faustus re-enters the stage with a pair of horns on his head, causing the Emperor to laugh that the Knight has "a wife, that not only gives thee horns,/ but makes thee wear them."[22] Again this is a very humorous scene, with the prop antlers highlighting the absurdity of the situation: "Always good for a laugh, the old antlers/cuckold gag."[23] Recent productions of *Merry Wives* have tended to opt for antlers rather than the full deer's head. For example, the 2024 production by the Royal Shakespeare Company saw Falstaff, played by John Hodgkinson, stick two large twigs into his cycling helmet to make his disguise. Herne's appearance is such an iconic moment of the play that it has come to define the play itself. Both the 1971 and 2000 Arden editions of *Merry Wives* have images of Herne the Hunter on the cover; the earlier edition giving a more traditional view while the 2000 edition has a man with his outstretched hands on his head representing the horns.

Once Sir John Falstaff has disguised himself as Herne he appears on stage and speaks a monologue filled with bestial imagery:

> The Windsor bell hath struck twelve, the minute draws on. Now the hot-blooded gods assist me! Remember, Jove, thou wast a bull for thy Europa; love set on thy horns. O powerful love, that in some respects makes a beast of man; in some other, a man, a beast! You were also, Jupiter, a swan for the love of Leda. O omnipotent love! How near a god drew to the complexion of a goose! A fault done first in the form of a beast – O Jove, a beastly fault! – and then another fault in the semblance of a fowl – think on't, Jove, a foul fault! When gods have hot backs, what shall poor men do? For me, I am here a Windsor stag, and the fattest, I think, I'th' forest. Send me a cool rut-time, Jove, or who can blame me to piss my tallow? (5.5.1-14)

Falstaff's speech includes references to both animals and gods, but is in no way elevated or divine. In fact, it is the opposite. The combining of human (or even godly) form with that of an animal is seen as a "foul fault." In the examples he gives, it is motivated by lust, which "makes a beast of a man ... a man, a beast." The reference at the end of the speech to pissing tallow relates to stags losing lots of weight because of their rutting. Here, Falstaff confesses he wishes to lose lots of weight through his vigorous love making.

As Mistress Page and Ford enter the stage, the animal imagery continues, as do the sexual innuendos:

> Sir John:
> Who comes here? My doe!
>
> Mistress Ford:
> Sir John! Art thou here, my deer, my male deer?
>
> Sir John:
> My doe with the black scut! ...
>
> Mistress Ford:
> Mistress Page is come with me, sweetheart.
>
> Sir John:
> Divide me like a bribed buck, each a haunch. I will keep my sides to myself, my shoulders for the fellow of this walk, and my horns I bequeath to your husbands. Am I a woodman, ha? Speak I like Herne the Hunter? (5.5.15-26)

After some light wordplay on the word deer, Falstaff makes the conversation bawdy by referring to Mistress Ford's "black scut," likely a reference to her pubic hair. Falstaff goes on to compare himself to a poached deer, being butchered and divided by those who have snared him, in this case, Mistresses Page and Ford. He completes the cuckolding joke by giving his horns to their husbands, clearly thinking he is about to sleep with their wives. He rounds off by asking if he convincingly resembles a woodman, a reference to a hunter but also a colloquial term for someone pursing a woman. "Speak I like Herne the Hunter?" he asks. Falstaff is always a provocative character but, once disguised as Herne, his language becomes filthy.

Of course, we need to consider the context here. Shakespeare is not presenting Herne the Hunter himself, but a lustful, bawdy character disguised as Herne as an act of humiliation by the women he is pursing. This is not the only time that Falstaff is degraded within the play – in Act 3, scene 3 he is bundled out of the way under a pile of dirty washing and in Act 4, scene 2 he makes his escape disguised as an old woman – but the fact that this is his final humiliation at the dénouement of the play implies this is the worst humiliation of them all. "Herne the Hunter" writes Harte "was not the epitome of forest majesty, but an example of how low you could stoop. We forget that times have changed: animality, which was once a foul reproach, is now rather popular. But, for Shakespeare and his contemporaries, anything that blurred the line between man and beast was disturbing and degrading."[24] This sense of degradation was not confined to the early modern period, when Shakespeare was writing. In fact, we see it in much earlier texts. For example, in the fourth branch of *The Mabinogion*, Gwydion and Gilfaethwy are turned into animals as punishment for their rape of Goewin:

> Then [Math] took his magic wand, and struck Gilfaethwy so that he changed into a good-sized hind, and he caught Gwydion quickly – he could not escape although he wanted to – and struck him with the same magic wand so that he changed into a stag.
>
> "Since you are in league with each other, I will make you live together and mate with each other, and take on the nature of the wild animals whose shape you are in..."[25]

This punishment is repeated three times, with Gwydion and Gilfaethwy being turned into wild boar and wolves in subsequent years. But it is Math's command that they will "take on the nature of the wild animals" which is crucial here, as the punishment is the same for Falstaff. Once in his horned costume, half-man, half-stag, the bestial aspects of Sir John's nature are presented, visually, to the audience:

> Falstaff is convinced that this disguise testifies to his prowess, and he imagines the 'pair of horns' (5.2.6) worn on his head align him with a 'bull' or a 'Windsor stag' (5.5.3,11) – symbols of virility. Yet the visual effect of the joke is to accentuate his domination by the wives of Windsor and his failure of sexual conquest.[26]

His degradation is inescapable for us and for the onstage inhabitants of Windsor. Falstaff is reduced to an animal, not elevated to a deity, which even he understands.

There is one last layer to this humiliation, a final part to the trick played on Falstaff by the Mistresses Ford and Page, which again makes Herne's horns central to the plot. Salingar writes that:

> More recent commentators have emphasised ... analogies with folk-customs enacting communal humiliation of sexual offenders. In particular, the final episode, where Falstaff is no longer simply the private butt of the merry wives but is intended to be 'publicly shamed' [IV.2.204-6], resembles the custom of the charivari or 'skimmington', widespread in the sixteenth century and persisting later, in which the offender could be represented in proxy by someone dressed up as a stag who was hunted down by a crowd of the neighbours, to the accompaniment of 'rough music' ... The story of Herne the Hunter and his oak is

> not genuine folklore ... It is introduced by Mrs Page as an 'idle headed superstition' [IV.4.25-35] which she and her friends can exploit so as to lure Falstaff with a misplaced sense of security into the park at midnight.[27]

Again, this leads us back to question of whether or not the story of Herne as presented in *Merry Wives* is authentic at all or whether it was created or heavily adapted by Shakespeare as a dramatic device, to get Falstaff to turn up to his own humiliation, willingly, carrying his own set of horns. To find a piece of local folklore about a horned ghost in Windsor would have been an incredible stroke of luck for Shakespeare, who plotted his play to end with custom that would have been quite common in provincial towns. Falstaff is publicly humiliated by the community and his friends, who are disguised as fairies and hobgoblins:

> Pinch him, and burn him and turn him about,
> Till candles and starlight and moonshine come out (5.5.100-101)

His humiliation complete, Falstaff's final line of the play drips with resignation:

> When night-dogs run, all sorts of deer are chased (5.5.230)

By closely examining the figure of Herne presented in *The Merry Wives of Windsor,* it has become clear that many of the attributes we associate with the figure, including his horns, are likely to be theatrical invention rather than an accurate reflection of a piece of local folklore. Does that mean that Shakespeare created Herne the Hunter from scratch and that there was no tradition of this story prior to 1597? No, not at all. But it does mean that we need to think carefully about just how far Shakespeare was involved in shaping and augmenting any possible story that was originally there.

This is why I wanted to begin this chapter with a discussion of the authorship of Shakespeare's plays, because, over the course of the last 400 years, we have seen similar yet opposing processes happening to William Shakespeare and Herne the Hunter.

We have plenty of evidence that the William Shakespeare, baptised in Stratford-upon-Avon on 26th April 1564 and who died in the town on 23rd April 1616, was the person who wrote the plays and poems ascribed to him. And yet, because we expect to have more documentary evidence, or because he did not leave explicitly personal writings, such as letters or diaries, or because we do not believe someone of his social standing from a small Warwickshire town could have had such a potent imagination, there are enough gaps for doubters to begin pulling at the threads and raising questions about his authorship.

For Herne the Hunter, the opposite is true. Here, a character based on a spurious piece of folklore, possibly created or, at the very least, heavily adapted by the playwright to help the dramatic outcome of their play, has been augmented with generation after generation of theory, assumption, and literary works which attempted to expand and develop his mythology. There are enough gaps in his folklore for us to fill them, somewhat convincingly, with ideas that he must have been an ancient deity. Herne must be an example of a Hunter god, we insist, because he has horns. But what if the horns were a creation of Shakespeare or a misunderstood part of the original oral tradition? As we will see in Chapter 3, some readers felt the horns mentioned in the play did not belong to Herne at all.

The more we have questioned the identity of the author of the play, the more certain we have become that Herne the Hunter has ancient roots – and all because, nowadays, we like filling in the gaps that we find in stories and making connections between ideas.

If Shakespeare did indeed just make Herne the Hunter up for the dénouement of his play, does that invalidate him as a legitimate deity? My answer may surprise you: no. Not at all. Just because Herne the Hunter does not have a line of evidenced worship stretching back to antiquity does not mean he is not a valid neo-Pagan god. In fact, in the rest of this book, I hope to show you the wonderful, magical process, woven over four centuries, which has made Herne the Hunter one of the predominant English deities.

To take the story further, we need to try looking for different sources of information. The character of Herne the Hunter presented in *The Merry Wives of Windsor* does not give us a clear view of any possible underlying folklore because it is so intricately connected with the internal, dramatic world of the play. After all, the play itself does hint that these other sources may exist. Mistress Page acknowledges the "superstitious idle-headed eld" who "Received and did deliver to our age / This tale of Herne the Hunter for a truth." (4.4.35-37). Is there any evidence in other documents of this oral tradition? And what about the oak tree Mistress Page mentions, which was clearly a local landmark within the play (a tree which, incidentally, isn't mentioned at all in the 1602 quarto version of the play)? In a drama which seems to have links to actual places within Windsor, and which would have been played to people who had some knowledge of the town, surely such an oak had to exist?

Well, maybe. But be warned, that man from Stratford is going to make things very confusing again.

Chapter 2

Ireland's Ghost

A Keeper of the Forest by Hannah Willow

Despite its royal connections and its castle, Windsor was a bit of a rural backwater in the 1600s. Shakespeare alludes to this several times in *The Merry Wives of Windsor*, where "The simplicity of the country people is a recurring theme" [1] The seeming lack of discernment and intelligence of the country folk is a source of amusement for the more cultured characters of the play and the audience. We can see this in the handling of the Herne the Hunter story within the play. Mistress Page sneers at the "superstitious idle-headed eld" (4.4.35) who have passed down the tale of Herne, while her husband notes there are still many people who find this somewhat silly legend terrifying:

> Why, yet there want not many that do fear
> In deep of night to walk by this Herne's Oak. (4.4.38-39)

It is the breadth of social classes, from peasant to royalty, which makes the play, its reception and Windsor itself so interesting. Early maps of Windsor tended to overlook the town itself and focused instead on the castle and the Great Park – in other words, the part of the town that the rich people, who could afford the maps, would frequent. But, in the early 1740s, that changed.

> William Collier's *Plan of the Town of and Castle of Windsor and Little Park and Town and College of Eton*, 1742, marks a big step forward in the cartography of Windsor. It is still primarily a map of the Castle and the Little Park, but the streets and houses of both Windsor and Eton are shown in fair detail. The map shows, amongst other things, how little the road pattern has changed over the centuries.[2]

The map, published according to an Act of Parliament, is important for another reason – it is the first time we see the setting of the final act of *The Merry Wives of Windsor*, where Falstaff is tricked beneath the boughs of Herne's Oak, marked on a map. Close to a long avenue of trees labelled as 'Queen Elizabeth's Walk' we find the site of Herne's Oak. Except it is not labelled as Herne's Oak on the map. It is called 'Sir John Falstaff's Oak.' This takes us back to the issue which haunted the entire first chapter of this book – was the story of Herne the Hunter a piece of local folklore which Shakespeare used within his play or was it simply something he created or, at least, heavily adapted? Collier's map hints that the location of the oak was commemorated for its connection to Shakespeare's play, rather than for its connection to any local piece of folklore.

It is important for us to understand what was happening with Shakespeare's works and his reputation, culturally, at the time. For us, Shakespeare is ubiquitous – he has always been part of our cultural world and probably always will be. But, for Windsorians and other people of culture in the 1740s,

Shakespeare's work was in the process of being 'restored' to its place of primacy in the literary canon. After Shakespeare's death, the country entered a period of political and spiritual turmoil which culminated in the English Civil Wars and the Protectorate of Oliver Cromwell, during which time much of Shakespeare's work was neglected: "The collected edition of his plays had not been reprinted since 1632. During the eighteen years between the official closing and reopening of the theatres, scores of old plays had been published ... but only three of Shakespeare's had even been reprinted."[3] With the restoration of Charles II in 1660, the country began to reshape itself and its culture, with Shakespeare at the heart of that process. "The first scholarly monograph devoted entirely to Shakespeare [was] published in 1726"[4] and shows just how the popularity of Shakespeare's works grew in the early part of the eighteenth century. *The Merry Wives of Windsor* "proved a very popular play to produce. It was produced over 200 times between 1700 and 1750."[5] The inclusion of 'Sir John Falstaff's Oak' on Collier's map is, therefore, a sign of the return to popularity of *The Merry Wives of Windsor* rather than something honouring of Herne himself. It was the re-emerging legacy of Shakespeare which ensured the continuation of Herne's story.

In the years after Collier's map, we find several drawings and engravings of the tree he labelled, although, in all cases it is called Herne's, rather than Falstaff's Oak. This suggests that Collier could either have mislabelled the tree or that, as more people began reading Shakespeare's plays again, they became used to calling it by the name it is given in *Merry Wives*. Perhaps the most striking of these pieces of art is by Alexander Cozens and was created between 1760 and 1780. It is a "pen and ink and wash drawing of the trunk and branch of a dead tree, identified by the artist on the mount as 'Hern[e]'s Oak in Windsor Park, mention'd in Shakespear[e]'s Merry Wives of Windsor'."[6] The thing that is so striking about this image is just how dead the tree looks. It is little more than a trunk, with a few bends in its single branch as it snakes upward. The bark is gnarled and looks ancient, the top is frayed and brittle, as if the upper branches have just snapped off. It really is an eerie and quite sad piece.

A lithograph of Herne's Oak by William Bromet[7] from 1777 shows a fuller tree, one with several branches, some even with leaves on them. The bark again looks ancient and gnarled and there are possibly some gaps or holes in the tree itself, hinting that the tree is hollow. It is possible to see the same contours to the tree as those in Cozens' piece, suggesting it could have been created before that image. There is a third small engraving of Herne's Oak, based upon an etching by Thomas Thornton[8], which was part of a book called *Shakespeare Illustrated*. The volume was a collection of images of Shakespeare and scenes from his plays which was collated by Silvester Harding. The image is dated to 1792, later than both images mentioned above, but seems to show an even fuller tree than those illustrated by Cozens and Bromet. The aspect which remains constant in all three versions is the dilapidation of the tree itself, with Thornton's piece seemingly showing a gaping, hollow centre of the trunk. Clearly drawn from the other side of the tree to Bromet's image, it is the most embellished of the three illustrations, with towering oaks in the background and three deer sheltering beneath the boughs. Both Thornton's and Bromet's oaks look much bigger than that drawn by Cozens, although, with its single branch and lack of background features, it is more difficult to judge the perspective of Cozens' tree.

The latter part of the eighteenth century saw "the growth period of English tourism,"[9] while the interest in Shakespeare and his connections with certain places also intensified. David Garrick's three-day Jubilee in Stratford-upon-Avon in 1769 is "widely credited as being a key moment in Stratford's history"[10] and the beginning of its role as a tourist destination for lovers of the Bard. There was clearly a similar movement going on in Windsor at the same time, with it celebrating its connection to Shakespeare and one of his most popular plays through Herne's Oak. A good example of this, and the next time we find Herne's name in print, came in 1792 with the publication of the snappily titled *Picturesque Views on the River Thames, from its source in Gloucestershire to the Nore: with Observations on the Public Buildings and Other Works of Art in its Vicinity, in 2 Volumes* by Samuel Ireland. This was the second guide book by Ireland, his first covering a tour through Holland and France, and later volumes covering other English rivers such as the Medway, Severn, and Avon.

If the name Samuel Ireland sounds familiar, then you might recall from Chapter 1 that it was his son, William Henry Ireland, who faked several documents, including the play *Vortigern,* which Samuel Ireland published as authentically by Shakespeare. Ireland was an enormous fan of the bard and it was his almost blind adoration of Shakespeare which was the source of his downfall. Patricia Pearce describes him as:

> ... a small, rotund man, pompous yet eager, and socially ambitious. He was full of contradictions: knowledgeable yet gullible, careful and meticulous, yet impetuous and reckless; vain but with an innocent childishness expressed in his obsession with collecting artefacts touched by fame, as he saw it. His obsessions turned into manias. There was the obsession with his collection of antiques linked to famous historical figures, with ancient books and, overriding all, his obsession with anything related to William Shakespeare, whose writings he didn't fully understand and frequently misquoted! Bernard Grebanier's assessment of him in a previous study is that he was 'less of an eighteenth-century rationalist than an agitated little chipmunk of a man.'[11]

Pierce goes further and claims that William Henry's forgeries were an attempt "simply to win the love and respect of his father,"[12] with whom he had a difficult relationship.

The Irelands visited Stratford-upon-Avon in 1793 to research the forthcoming *Picturesque views of the Avon*, and Samuel fully immersed himself in the tall stories he was told and even bought several objects supposedly related to Shakespeare which he found there. William Henry "had seen his father duped at every turn in Stratford"[13] and, Pierce suggests, it was this gullibility which led him to begin forging documents. We need to bear this in mind when considering Samuel Ireland's presentation of information about Herne the Hunter in *Picturesque Views of the River Thames* (1792), because the same mania which made him susceptible to being "duped" in Stratford could have led to him being misled in Windsor.

Ireland gives a short but interesting account of the tale of Herne the Hunter, although it is repeatedly overlaid by his fawning attitude to Shakespeare. "The north terrace of [Windsor] castle was greatly improved by Queen Elizabeth..." Ireland begins. "Not far from this place are the remains of that venerable tree, known by the name of Herne's Oak, which has been immortalized by our divine bard Shakespeare in his Merry Wives of Windsor."[14] Notice Ireland's language here. The oak is deemed to be "venerable," meaning it is worthy of great respect either because of its great age or because it potentially has some spiritual significance. In this case, however, that link to the spiritual comes through Shakespeare and not Herne. It is the "divine" playwright that has "immortalised" the tree. There may be some truth in this; after all, it was the renewed interest in Shakespeare's plays which would have led to people visiting the spot, but Ireland's gushing language is over the top and cloying.

After quoting from the play, Ireland continues: "The story of Herne, who was a keeper of the forest in the time of Elizabeth, runs thus: That having committed some great offence, for which he feared to lose his situation, and fall into disgrace, he was induced to hang himself on this tree."[15]

What is really interesting here is that Ireland presents us with new information, that Herne hung himself on the oak tree, which is not drawn from Shakespeare's play. This must, therefore, have come from some other, possibly local, source he encountered while researching the river. The key thing to notice here is that Ireland claims that Herne was a keeper during the time of Elizabeth I's reign. This means that, if Ireland is to be believed, the story of Herne would not have been passed down by the "superstitious idle-headed eld" (4.4.35) as claimed in *Merry Wives*, but would have been roughly contemporaneous with the writing of the play.

Shakespeare offers no reason why Herne's ghost haunts a particular tree, while Ireland asserts that Herne hung himself on its branches, because of some scandal, to which we are not made party. Herne hanging himself on the oak would certainly give him reason to haunt it. However, Ireland is somewhat scornful of the whole ghost story:

> The credulity of the times easily worked on the minds of the ignorant to suppose that his ghost should haunt the spot. This rendered it a fit scene of action of the purpose for our bard to terrify and expose the cowardice of the fat knight ...[16]

Ireland here seems to give us an answer to that question about whether Shakespeare made up the tale of Herne or whether he used a piece of local folklore. For Ireland, the answer is, emphatically, the latter.

Especially interesting here is that Ireland makes no reference to Herne having horns at all. That part of the story is glossed in this account, possibly because, through an increase in number of performances and people reading the play, Herne's horns were such an inbuilt and accepted part of his appearance that they did not need to be mentioned.

Ireland, usefully, provides an illustration of the oak for his readers: "As I do not know any engraving has been made of this tree, the annexed view may possibly afford some pleasure to the curious reader."[17] Again, this does raise some questions about just how widely Ireland researched the subject as there had been several engravings made of the tree before he published his book. Ireland's drawing does share some similarities with those by Bromet and Thornton, although Ireland places Windsor Castle in the background and seemingly has Mistresses Page and Ford accompanying Sir John on an afternoon walk beneath its branches – Ireland here begins a tradition which would appear on many illustrations of Herne's oak over the next centuries. His account of the Herne's Oak finishes with a rather ominous tone: "Some idea has prevailed of an intention to cut down this celebrated tree, which it is much to be wished may not be true. The dell near it has in part been recently filled up."[18]

Unfortunately, in this case, Ireland was somewhat prophetic and it seems that Herne's Oak did not last much longer. In 1796 it was, apparently, felled by the order of King George III:

> Mr. Charles Knight considers that the real Herne's Oak was cut down some fifty or sixty years ago, not by order of George III., but to his deep and lasting regret; ... Lady Ely informed Mr. Nicholson that she had made the inquiry he wished of the king; who told her that, when he (George III.) was a young man, it was represented to him that there were a number of old oaks in the park, which had become unsightly objects, and that it would be desirable to take them down. He gave immediate directions that such trees as were of this description should be removed;

> but he was afterwards sorry that he had given such an order inadvertently, because he found that among the rest the remains of Herne's Oak had been destroyed.[19]

From the rumours that Ireland heard on his visit, and the state of the tree as shown in several engravings at the time, it is little wonder that Herne's Oak was felled when this order was given.

However, the felling of the tree was still something of a scandal and was prompted a particularly insightful outpouring of grief in the form of poetry. The following piece, named *Upon Herne's Oak being cut down, in the spring of 1796,* was written by one Mr Thomas Wright and published in *The Whitehall Evening Herald*:

> Within this dell, for many an age,
> Herne's Oak uprear'd its antique head:—
> Oh! most unhallow'd was the rage
> Which tore it from its native bed!
>
> The storm that stript the forest bare
> Would yet refrain this tree to wrong,
> And Time himself appear'd to spare
> A fragment he had known so long.
>
> 'Twas mark'd with popular regard,
> When famed Elizabeth was queen;
> And Shakespere, England's matchless bard,
> Made it the subject of a scene.
>
> So honour'd when in verdure drest,
> To me the wither'd trunk was dear;
> As, when the warrior is at rest,
> His trophied armour men revere.

That nightly Herne walk'd round this oak,
"The superstitious eld received;"
And what they of his outrage spoke
The rising age in fear believ'd.

The hunter, in his morning range,
Would not the tree with lightness view:
To him Herne's legend, passing strange,
In spite of scoffers still seem'd true.

Oh, where were all the fairy crew
Who revels kept in days remote,
That round the oak no spell they drew,
Before the axe its fibres smote?

Could wishes but ensure the power,
The tree again its head should rear;
Shrubs fence it with a fadeless bower,
And these inscriptive lines appear:—

"Here, as wild Avon's poet stray'd"—
Hold!—let me check this feeble strain—
The spot by Shakspere sacred made,
A verse like mine would but profane![20]

Mr Wright's poem provides us with some valuable information. It gives us a reason for why Herne's Oak looks so battered and broken in the illustrations from the time – it seems to have been damaged in a storm which "stript the forest bare," with the personification of "Time" keeping a "fragment" of it safe. Wright feels the tree, rather than simply being decrepit, is "like a warrior at rest," its bark being its armour. Wright also clearly dates the story of Herne to a time before Queen Elizabeth, here differing with Ireland. By Elizabeth's reign, "Time" had already intervened and saved the tree which was then held in "popular regard." Here, again, is an answer to the question about whether Shakespeare invented Herne or not and, again, Mr Wright suggests that the story of Herne is a piece of local folklore which Shakespeare used rather than something he made up. Wright advocates for the supernatural aspect of the tree, with the hunters of the park knowing the story of Herne's ghost to be true, while "scoffers," like Samuel Ireland, simply do not understand. Here is also another connection between Herne and fairies, developing Shakespeare's fake fairies from the final scene of *Merry Wives*, with Wright wishing that real fairies would have cast some protection on the tree against the axes which felled it.

But, once again, it is the tree's connection with Shakespeare and his play which made it so very special. Shakespeare is portrayed as "England's matchless bard" and, just as we see in Ireland's account, it is Shakespeare, the "divine bard,"[21] who made the tree a sacred spot, not Herne. Rather than a deity, Herne is the ghost of a human, although it appears that Shakespeare himself has been elevated to such a degree that he almost a god.

With the oak gone, the story of Herne could easily have died out. But the tale of a keeper who haunts Windsor Great Park, sporting a pair of horns, was to have a certain Grimm fascination in the nineteenth century. A sensational novel would move Herne away from Shakespeare's influence and place him firmly into the public imagination, so much so that many of the facts we think we know about Herne come from a single, thrilling piece of fiction.

Chapter 3

Ainsworth's Demon

The Wild Hunter by Hannah Willow

On the last day of August 1863, Herne's Oak was felled, again, this time in a storm.

I am sure that you are wondering how a tree which had been cut down on the instructions of King George III in 1796 could have fallen over *again* over half a century later. The answer is that, during the intervening period, a completely different tree had been identified as Herne's Oak by several people of note, including Queen Victoria herself. The debate about which tree was the original to bear the name of Herne's Oak became so fraught, so contentious, that Victoria commissioned a thorough investigation into the authenticity of the two trees, a task entrusted to her own trusted woodcarver, William Perry.

The result of Perry's investigation is one of the most intriguing documents connected to Herne the Hunter. It is called *A Treatise on the identity of Herne's Oak, shewing the Maiden Tree to have been the Real One* (1867). A Maiden Tree, such as the one felled in 1863, is "a tree of seedling origin which has never been coppiced or pollarded"[1]. The other tree, felled in 1796, is referred to in the text simply as "the old pollard,"[2] making the two trees quite distinct from each other.

Perry's investigation is incredibly thorough and he sifts through much evidence, such as that presented in the last chapter. He mentions Samuel Ireland and his claim that the legend of Herne the Hunter dates from the time of Queen Elizabeth, only to point that the "authority for that statement we know not."[3] Perry also takes Shakespeare's writing literally, identifying actual geographical features from the words of the characters, stating that while:

> I am quite aware, that to this reasoning some will object, and say, the play was written to be performed on a stage, and therefore these minor points, as they may call them, are of no moment. ... nevertheless, I understand that Shakespeare made himself acquainted with all the localities mentioned in the play, and acted it before a Windsor audience, and therefore believe that his good sense would prompt him to adopt such performances, as were most consistent, with the peculiar features of the places represented.[4]

Ultimately Perry comes down on the side of the Maiden Tree being the authentic Herne's Oak, which is lucky for him, considering that he had been given several bits of the tree by the Queen to make into glorious artefacts. Yes, just as Perry reveals the results of his investigation, it becomes clear just how biased he actually is:

> The reader will, perhaps, be pleased to know that a Casket, designed and executed by the Author, to encase an exceedingly fine copy of the rare first folio edition of Shakespeare's Comedies, Histories and Tragedies, and the first collected edition of his Poems, has been made from the wood of this venerable tree, for Miss Burdett Coutts: the wood having been very graciously granted by her majesty the Queen for that purpose.[5]

He also appears to have carved a bust of Shakespeare from the wood of the same tree which also passed through the hands of royalty[6]. The defining piece of evidence for Perry seems to relate to a story about George III, who when presented with three chairs made from the tree felled in 1796 and told they were made from Herne's Oak, indicated the Maiden Tree and said that Herne's tree was still standing. Just in case any readers worry about the validity of the notably 'mad' George's testimony, Perry points out that the event happened ten years before the King's "incapacity"[7].

While Perry's conclusions are problematic (Jane Roberts in her book *Royal Landscape* states that the Maiden Tree was "probably mistakenly"[8] identified as Herne's Oak) it his wider comments on the tale of Herne the Hunter which are far more interesting.

The first such comment comes early in the text where he states what Samuel Ireland only inferred – that Herne's Oak is only of interest because of its connection to Shakespeare, not because of the story of Herne himself:

> The interest felt in this venerable tree, as the reader is aware, arises not so much from an old tradition having been connected with it, as from its having been incorporated with that tradition into one of the plays of Shakespeare, and made the theatre of a very humorous scene in that play.[9]

In fact, by the end of the book, Perry states that the tree was likely noteworthy before Shakespeare's play or any story of Herne became attached to it: "My opinion is, that the tradition of Herne the Hunter was not the cause of the oak first being held in estimation, but the consequence of it having been previously esteemed."[10]

He goes further, noting the size and shape of the tree and proposing that "the tree was used by keepers as a place of shelter long before the tradition was attached to it."[11] The Maiden Tree, Perry suggests, would have been of great use to keepers as a source of shelter:

> Before the trees around it were lopped, this was noticed [by keepers] as the best adapted for shelter; and so, when the other trees were lopped in the winter for the deer to feed upon the bark, when the ground was covered with snow this was preserved by the foresters or keepers for the sake of their own shelter in the summer ... and it became a favourite haunt for them.[12]

This is such an interesting suggestion, that the connection between Herne and the tree could spring not from a great tragedy or "some great offence"[13] but from the fact that the tree had been long associated with working keepers.

Perry does, however, try to track down the age of the myth surrounding Herne. He rejects Ireland's suggestion that it dates from Elizabethan times and instead relies upon the work of one of the great Shakespeareans of the era: James Orchard Halliwell-Phillipps. In the 1860s, Halliwell-Phillipps led the excavation of Shakespeare's home, New Place, in Stratford-upon-Avon but was also noted for his work on Shakespeare's life and plays. In 1842, Halliwell-Phillipps had published *The First Sketch of Shakespeare's Merry Wives of Windsor*, which was essentially an edition of the 1602 quarto text with introductory notes and appendices. In it, he identifies a possible source for the Herne myth, where the difference textual variation between the 1602 and 1623 texts plays an important role:

> Before I conclude these brief introductory observations, there is one point I wish to introduce to the reader's notice, though I will not pretend to say how far I may be borne out in my opinion. It is a singular fact that no allusion to the legend of Horne the Hunter, as he is called in the following sketch, has ever been discovered in any other writer. We are entirely ignorant of the date of the legend. In a manuscript, however of the time of Henry VIII., in the British Museum, I find "Rycharde Horne, yeoman" among "the names of the hunters whiche be examynde and have confessed" for hunting in his majesty's forests. Is it improbable to suppose that this was the person to whom the tale related by Mistress Page alludes?[14]

You will remember that the 1602 quarto edition refers to the character as Horne the Hunter throughout, making the joke about cuckoldry much more obvious. It also, rather convincingly, links the figure to "Rycharde Horne, yeoman" which Halliwell-Phillipps found in the historical record. Perry certainly thought so, writing: "I think it is not improbable..."[15] and that "there appears no evidence of Herne the Hunter having existed at an earlier date than Henry VIII..."[16]

To consolidate the idea that the story of Herne may have been a relatively recent event prior to the writing of the play and not an ancient myth, Halliwell-Phillipps turns to the text of the 1602 edition, which is significantly different to the later folio text. There is no sense that the story is part of an oral tradition in the 1602 version, it is not passed down by the "superstitious idle-headed eld" (4.4.33). Halliwell-Phillipps notes that Mistress Page "speaks of him as no very ancient personage" simply stating "Oft have you heard since Horne the hunter died."[17] Perry concurs but relies on personal experience rather than textual analysis to make his point:

> It appears scarcely likely that such a tradition would have been handed down for two whole centuries orally. We can remember, when children, hearing tales of like import told by our grandsires; we have now only an imperfect recollection of them, so faint, indeed, that they are not likely to be transmitted to our posterity, even if we had faith in them: therefore, we can put some limits in our minds, as to the probable time Herne lived.[18]

After dealing with Halliwell-Phillipps, Perry turns his attention to another of the eras great Shakespeareans, Charles Knight, mentioned in the previous chapter because of his knowledge of George III's reaction to the felling of the older tree. This time, Perry is less than supportive of Knight's idea. To be fair to Perry, Knight's reading of the text of *The Merry Wives of Windsor* has not been adopted by any subsequent editors of the play, but its impact to the figure of Herne could be profound.

Charles Knight was a Windsor-born publisher, known for his work on *The Pictorial Shakspere* alongside several other almanacs and magazines. Knight's Windsor pedigree gives an interesting twist to the tale which Perry recounts and the tree he identified as Herne's Oak:

> "Mr Knight, having describe his earliest recollections of the locality in which Herne's Oak stood, says, – 'Five or six years later we came to look for the "Oak with great ragg'd horns" to which we had been introduced by Shakespeare.' This rendering of the passage is calculated to lead any careless reader into error."[19]

Just pause for one second after reading that quotation and consider the profound change that Knight suggests. When Mistress Page suggests that "Herne the Hunter ... Doth all the winter-time, at still midnight, / Walk round about an oak, with great ragg'd horns;" (4.4.25-28) Knight suggests that she means that the oak tree has the horns and NOT Herne.

Of course, Knight has got this wrong, within the context of the play. The fact that Mistress Quickly says she will find some horns for Falstaff and that the horns on Falstaff's head are central to the action and humour of the play, means that the horns *have* to be on Herne's head. However, it is truly astonishing to stop and pause for a second to think that Herne's current reputation could be based on a misreading of the text or, possibly, a deliberate distortion of the original folklore by Shakespeare, to suit the needs of his play. What if the elderly Knight was remembering a piece of the original Windsor oral folklore connected to Herne? What if Knight's account is more faithful to the original Herne story than what we have inferred since, because Shakespeare changed it?

Within the context of Perry's work, Knight's words are used to give validity to the tree cut down in 1796, "the old pollard"[20], which Perry is keen to discredit. The fragmented nature of that tree could mean that, to some onlookers, it could be considered to have had "ragg'd horns." Perry dismisses this entirely. He says that Knight's idea is "a glaring misquotation, and renders his evidence of on this subject very doubtful quality."[21] But that conclusion does not appease Perry and he comes back to Knight to disparage him again later in the book, in a piece of writing which is incredibly pertinent for the way we perceive Herne today:

> This was an error easily to be made in youth, especially if the branches of the tree at all resembled 'ragg's horns;'

> which they probably did, at least to his young fresh mind. I refer to this, not for the purpose of showing up Mr Knight's error, or wishing to detract one iota from his great and well-merited reputation. My only object is to show how easily a wrong notion is formed in our mind in youth, and how tenaciously it will cling to us, or we to it, in maturer years, even if the very best and brightest.[22]

What Perry suggests here is that we, as humans, can misremember things, and that misremembering can shape our approach to subjects later in life. I think it is important we carry Perry's words with us as we continue this journey. The current neo-Pagan view of Herne is very different to any version of him we have encountered in this journey so far. Are we like Knight? Do we have "a wrong notion [that] is formed in our mind in youth" which we have carried with us? And if so, is that necessarily a bad thing?

Perry's *Treatise* is a thoroughly interesting review of the evidence surrounding Herne's Oak. Like Ireland, his work is of value, despite its obvious bias. He is not looking to embroider a narrative, he is trying to make a case about the status of a particular tree. What this means is that he refers to the ideas of those who disagree with him, such as Knight (and, incidentally, Halliwell-Phillipps, who advocates for the 1796 tree at the end of his *Sketch*). These contrasting views give us an important sense of the wider discussion about the story of Herne in the mid-nineteenth century.

The response to the felling of the Maiden Tree was not all so well thought out and reasoned, though. There is a wonderful tale that Queen Victoria herself was so overwhelmed by the loss of the tree that she led the nation in a period of national mourning. As glorious as this tale is, it is now felt to be apocryphal[23]. And, just as in 1796, the felling of Herne's Oak in

1863 was the source for an outpouring of extended poetry. The following poem, called *Herne's Oak,* was written by T. Nason, which is reprinted here with permission from the Windsor Local History Group:

Through Windsor's Park there goes a tale
About an old oak tree.
Which, like most others of its kind,
Is wrapt in mystery.

When storms do rage and fierce winds howl
At dismal dark midnight,
Through Winter's time there may be seen
A curious spectral sight,

Of Herne, who once the chase had led
Through many a brake and dell
No hunter then in all the land,
His prowess could excel.

And so he led the Royal pack,
Till an unlucky thing –
He great displeasure did create
With Harry, who was King.

Being dismissed from service good,
Which followed speedily,
The tale is told he hung himself
Upon this huge oak tree.

And so at Winter's dark midnight
His figure might be seen,
Together with his spectral hounds,
Come rushing o'er the green.

The tree they say would open wide
Amid the raging storms,
To enclose within its hollow trunk
These fiery demon forms.

The famous bard of Avon, too,
Immortalized this tree
With The Merry Wives of Windsor
And their glorious jollity.

Sir John Falstaff and fairy elves
Did sport around the same,
When Herne appeared with monstrous horns
Amid the smoke and flame.

Some years have passed since Shakespeare wrote,
And changes there have been
The tree is gone, and others too –
Quite altered is the scene

For age has felled its ancient stem,
Assisted by the blast,
And leaves it but a shattered wreck –
A relic of the past.

But remnants of this dear old trunk
In Windsor shall be seen,
Preserved by Windsor's merry maids,
To say what it has been.

Our noble Queen, too, has been pleased
To humbly ascertain—
Now it's so suddenly removed
From off her Royal domain—

To best preserve the remnants
Of this old curious tree,
Till dust shall finish all that's left
With our posterity.

So it's to grace the Castle fair,
And doubtless there will be
Admired by every Royal one
For many a century

And till the last they'll tell the tale
About Herne's Haunted Tree,
Sir John FALSTAFF, the MERRY WIVES,
And SHAKESPEARE'S memory.[24]

We find much in Nason's poem which comes direct from *The Merry Wives of Windsor,* including that Herne appears at midnight in the winter time and a brief account of the trick played upon Falstaff (which is augmented with "smoke and flame"). The poem ends by restating the claim we have heard so often, that Herne's Oak is a monument to the genius of Shakespeare and not Herne himself. But, while respectful reference is made to Shakespeare throughout the poem, the fawning hero-worship we find in so many texts from the 1700s is absent. By 1863, Shakespeare's reputation and place in British culture was secure, so it is possible that the author did not feel the need to be so ebullient in their praise.

However, there is also an awful lot of content in this poem which does not come from Shakespeare's play. By the time the Maiden Tree fell and Nason committed his thoughts to paper, Herne's tale was beginning to change and develop, picking up aspects from different contributors. We get references to Queen Victoria's concern for the tree and, possibly, a hint that Perry had been commissioned to undertake his study when the poem was being composed. Halliwell-Phillipp's evidence that Herne's story originated in the time of Henry VIII is repeated here and is linked to Ireland's claim that the keeper hung himself from the tree.

Nason also refers to a series of more chilling, demonic elements. Herne, we are told, used to lead a chase with "the Royal pack," which take the form of "spectral hounds" by the end of the poem. The trunk of Herne's Oak opens to hide "These fiery demon forms." Nothing we have encountered so far hints at such a tradition. So where does this come from?

The roots of this more sinister aspect, particularly those involving a pack of spectral dogs, can be traced back to 1835 when Jacob Grimm, one of the famous storytelling brothers, published his seminal work *Deutsche Mythologie.* Originally published in Grimm's native German, it was not published in English (as *Teutonic Mythology*) until the 1880s, although its influence can clearly be seen in Nason's 1863 poem. In *Deutsche Mythologie,* Grimm outlines what he calls the Wilde Jagd or Wild Hunt:

> Another class of spectres ... instead of straggling singly on the earth as fires, they sweep through forest and air in whole companies with a horrible din. This is the widely spread legend of the furious host, the furious hunt, which is of high antiquity, and interweaves itself, now with gods, and now with heroes.[25]

Danu Forest gives an excellent contemporary account of the Wild Hunt as "a pan-European tradition ... [which] functions as a vast energetic wave sweeping across the land, clearing away the dead and any unwelcome spirits, although it is also a subject of fear as an example of chthonic forces literally upending the normal structure and riding either across the land or in the sky bringing change, retribution for misdeeds or general chaos to the mortal world."[26] When turning his attention to British participants in the Wild Hunt, Grimm mentions "King Arthur's mighty Hunt"[27] and also Herne the Hunter, who, he notes is a deity that "had got localized."[28]

And that is it. With a single mention of Herne's name and some quoted lines from Shakespeare, Grimm elevated Herne from a ghost that circled a tree to a deity and leader of the Wild Hunt. It is probably the most significant development in his mythology since Shakespeare's original play. The consequences of his inclusion in Grimm's work were to change the course of Herne's history. We can see that, by 1863 it had armed him, in the popular imagination with a horde of spectral hounds and freed him from the immediate vicinity of the oak (although he still returns to it at the end of his hunt).

There can be no doubt about the quality of Grimm's work. *Deutsche Mythologie* is a vitally important and respected academic investigation. But was his inclusion of Herne as a participant or even a leader of the Wild Hunt, correct? There is certainly nothing in the documentary evidence we have seen so far that would suggest he was involved in such a supernatural event. The only possible link between Herne and the Wild Hunt is his name. He is, after all, a hunter. So, should we take this, alone, as evidence that he was an ancient deity who would have led a spectral chase? Not everyone is convinced, and among those voices is Ronald Hutton, who does not believe the attribution is secure. In his article *The Wild Hunt and the Witches' Sabbath,* Hutton argues that "the modern notion of the 'Hunt' was created by Jacob Grimm, who conflated different medieval traditions with modern folklore."[29] When applying a new approach to attributions of involvement in the Wild Hunt to early modern texts, Hutton argues that:

> Nobody associated [Herne] with the Hunt until Grimm suggested that he might have been an English version of

> its leader (because of his name) ... More fundamentally, the methodology adopted here also renders the very term 'Wild Hunt' as irrelevant as Herne, because its adoption by scholars was entirely due to its prominence in modern German folklore. As Lecouteux has shown, medieval and early modern sources refer to three different kinds of spectral huntsman: a demon, chasing sinners; a sinful human huntsman, condemned to roam without rest as a penance; and a wild man who chases otherworldly prey and sometimes human livestock (Lecouteux 2011, 56-84). None usually has a retinue, of the living or the dead, and so are not aspects of what the Wild Hunt was later taken to be.[30]

Grimm's attribution of a role in the Wild Hunt to Herne was, at best, brief. Within the enormous three volume work, Herne gets little more than a sentence and a footnote. And yet the effect of those few lines fundamentally shifted the trajectory of Herne's mythology. Is it possible that Grimm's book alone was responsible for this? Respected as it was, *Deutsche Mythologie* was hardly going to reach a wide readership and gain much traction in popular culture. For that to happen, Grimm's idea would need to be picked up and disseminated in a different, more accessible way. And that is exactly what happened.

In the words of his biographer, Stephen Carter, "William Harrison Ainsworth is the national treasure that most people haven't heard of."[31] Ainsworth's name is not one that pops up on syllabuses of English Literature. Many of his books are not even in print anymore, with second hand or facsimile copies being the only way that modern readers can engage with his work. But just because we do not really know of him today does not mean we should underestimate his influence on the audience of the nineteenth century:

> An energetic and prolific author, Ainsworth wrote and published well over a hundred literary articles and short stories, two volumes of poetry, and forty (mostly) historical novels, fictionalising four centuries of British history. In his heyday, Ainsworth commanded a massive audience, if not always critical acclaim, his novels multiply adapted for the stage and plagiarised by the penny-a-liners.[31]

And it was Ainsworth who picked up on Grimm's version of Herne the Hunter as the leader of the Wild Hunt and wove it into a compelling narrative in his 1842 novel *Windsor Castle*. It is this version of Herne, this novel, which was absorbed into the British cultural imagination and changed Herne from a ghost circling a single tree into a figure leading a Wild Hunt.

It might seem odd that a novel most people have never heard of by a man they have never heard of can have shaped our view of Herne the Hunter so profoundly. But, according to Carver, Ainsworth's work is responsible for having shaped the response of the British psyche to several folkloric and mythological figures, so much so that his sensational literary embellishments are now simply accepted as facts. As evidence for this, Carter lists a number of twentieth century film and television versions of Dick Turpin, claiming that "all of these modern portrayals of Turpin ultimately lead back to *Rookwood*", Ainsworth's gothic romance of 1834, "which in turn goes back to Ainsworth's childhood."[32] Similarly, Carter examines our modern approach to Guy Fawkes and how it was shaped by Alan Moore's *V for Vendetta*: "...while the cultural significance of Moore's subversive hero is huge, the connotative seed of Guy Fawkes as a revolutionary freedom fighter, rather than a terrorist to be burnt in effigy, were in fact sown in Ainsworth's novel," *The Tower of London*.[33]

So how does Ainsworth present Herne in *Windsor Castle*? Well, at the start of the novel, it feels like his characterisation is lifted straight out of Shakespeare's play, albeit with some spectacular gothic twists. Chapter 1 sees the Earl of Surrey admiring Home Park in Windsor where he is warned: "Only let me caution you against going near Herne's Oak. It is said that the demon-hunter walks at nightfall, and scares, if he does not injure, all those who cross his path."[34] Despite scoffing at the warning, mere pages later Surrey finds himself encountering the legendary figure:

> Suddenly, however, he was startled by a blue phosphoric light streaming through the bushes on the left, and, looking up, he beheld at the foot of an enormous oak whose giant roots protruded like twisted snakes from the bank, a wild, spectral-looking object possessing some slight resemblance to humanity, and habited, so far as it could be determined, in the skins of deer, strangely disposed about its gaunt and tawny coloured limbs. On its head was seen a sort of helmet formed of the skull of a stag, from which branched a pair of large antlers; from its left arm hung a heavy and rusty-looking chain, in the links of which burned the phosphoric fire before mentioned; while on its right wrist was perched a large horned owl, with feathers erected and red, staring eyes.[35]

Herne even begins "circling the tree, and blasting it"[36] an action lifted straight from Shakespeare's dialogue.

But that is where the similarities between Shakespeare's characterisation and Ainsworth's demon-hunter end. For Ainsworth, Herne is no mere plot device. Instead, he emerges as the principal antagonist of the novel, involved in every plot and subplot, whether they be romantic or historical. Just when the action threatens to become dull, Herne appears with a flourish. He is clearly a supernatural figure, referred to variously as a "demon,"[37] an "infernal spirit,"[38] a "false fiend,"[39] and a "spectral huntsman."[40] His appearance often coincides with thunder and lightning, another sure sign of his infernal intent. He is so bold, so brash, he even stands up to the notoriously cantankerous figure of Henry VIII, saying: "Welcome to my domain, Harry of England. You are lord of the castle but I am lord of the forest. Ha! Ha!"[41] His self-proclaimed title as "lord of forest" is one that would follow him into the twentieth century and beyond.

While Ainsworth's Herne often looks as we would expect, with his horned helmet and chain, there is also something deeply animalistic about his physical form. On one occasion in the novel, when he is hunting a deer, he gets down on all fours and engages in a brief but startling tussle with the animal:

> Drawing a knife from his girdle, the hunter threw himself on the ground, and, advancing on all fours towards the hart, could scarcely be distinguished himself from some denizen of the forest. As he approached, the hart snorted and bellowed fiercely, and dashed its horns against him; but the blow was received by the hunter upon his own antlered helm, and at the same moment his knife was thrust to the hilt into the stag's throat, and it fell to the ground.[42]

Even when not crawling around on all fours, Herne is terrifying. We are told that "His appearance was so terrific and unearthly that they all shrank aghast"[43] and that "His giant frame dilated; his eyes flashed fire; and the expression of his countenance was so fearful that" even one of his closest allies "shielded his eyes with his hands."[44]

Ainsworth's Herne is also tremendously skilled. Beyond the obviously talents he has in hunting, he can conjure visions, has a great range of disguises (including that of a friar with "a diabolic grin"[45] who appears near the end of the novel to Anne Boleyn) and can even disappear in a puff of "sulphurous smoke."[46] Herne can also predict the future and saves his gravest warning for Henry VIII. "But now mark me, Harry of England, thou fierce and bloody king! – thou shall be drunken with the blood of thy wives; and thy end shall be a fearful one ... and when dead, the very hounds with which thou huntedst me shall lick thy blood!"[47]

Herne appears to Henry again, close to the end of the novel, warning him he is "on the eve of committing a great crime."[48] As Anne Boleyn is executed and Herne's prophecies come true, he appears one final time to finish the novel:

> "There spoke the death-knell of Anne Boleyn!" cried Herne, regarding Henry sternly, and pointing to the Round Tower. "The bloody deed is done, and thou art free to wed once more. Away to Wolff Hall and bring thy new consort to Windsor Castle!"[49]

Ainsworth is the first writer to separate Herne from a single location, his oak, and give him several different domains and realms to inhabit. Herne's Oak does appear several times throughout the novel, but Ainsworth connects Herne to several other trees in the park too, including a "beech-tree near the marsh."[50] At one point, another Oak into which Herne disappears is cut down, the roots being excavated and burned in an unsuccessful attempt to catch him. Herne regularly pops up inside Windsor Castle and out on its battlements. Water is also an important conduit for Herne, who can disappear into one of the lakes in the park:

> As the wild huntsman reached the brink of the lake, he placed a horn to his mouth, and blew from it a bright blue flame, which illuminated his own dusky and hideous features, and shed a wild and unearthly glimmer over the surrounding objects. While enveloped in this flame, the

> demon plunged into the lake, and apparently descended to its abysses...[51]

Ainsworth also creates a spectacular subterranean lair for Herne, where many crucial scenes take place:

> The roof, which might be about ten feet high, was supported by the trunks of three large trees ... On the right hand stood a pile of huge stones, disposed somewhat in the form of a Druidical altar, on the top of which, as on a throne, sat the demon-hunter, surrounded by his satellites – one of whom, horned and bearded like a satyr...[52]

Herne's "cavalcade"[53] of followers is striking. In Shakespeare's play, Herne is a lonely spirit who frightens other people away, not someone who gathers an entourage around him. Ainsworth's novel is the first time we see references to him having "satellites," linking to Grimm's idea that he had a role in leading others.

This means that, long before *Deutsche Mythologie,* was translated into English, Ainsworth took Grimm's idea that Herne is a leader of the Wild Hunt and developed it as a central part of his novel. His myriad readers would have found this to be one of the most compelling and exciting aspects of the story, which is possibly the reason why it became a central part of his mythos in the popular imagination. The novel is filled with adrenaline-fuelled chases around Windsor:

> And he pointed to a weird-looking figure, mounted on a steed, as weird looking as itself, galloping through the trees with extraordinary swiftness, at a little distance from them. The ghostly rider wore the antlered helmet described by Surrey, and seemed to be habited in a garb

> of deer skins. Before him flew a large owl, and a couple of great black dogs ran beside him.[54]

We later find out that his hounds are called "Saturn and Dragon,"[55] further indications of Herne's fiery, hellish persona. It is not only animals which join Herne in hunting. Ainsworth tells us of "a number of wild figures in fantastic garbs, some mounted on swarthy steeds and accompanied by hounds, others on foot"[56] who join the hunt, although some of these turn out to be less fantastical than the satyr in his cave. Many of Herne's Hunters are, in fact, very human.

Herne's interactions with many of the human characters in the novel represents "Ainsworth's continuing interest in the Faustian pact,"[57] where someone is seen to sell their soul to the devil to get their heart's desire: "... people do say that Morgan Fenwolf is in league with the devil – or with Herne the hunter, which is the same thing."[58] By putting Herne into the Devil's position in this interaction, Ainsworth makes Herne's evil nature clear to his readers, but also elevates Herne in terms of the amount of power he has. He is no longer a figure blasting a single tree but one which can invade castle bedrooms to promise his victims everything they ever desired. Readers get to witness the character of Thomas Wyat being seduced by Herne over the first part of the novel. Wyat wants to win back Anne Boleyn from Henry VIII:

> "I would give my soul to win her back from my kingly rival," cried Wyat.
>
> "I accept your offer," rejoined the spirit. "Anne Boleyn shall be yours. Your hand upon the compact."
>
> Wyat stretched forth his hand, and grasped that of the demon. His fingers were compressed, as if by a vice, and he felt himself dragged towards the tree, while a stifling and sulphurous vapour rose around him. A black veil fell over his head, and was rapidly twined around his brow,

> in thick folds. Amid yells of fiendish laughter, he was then lifted from the ground, and thrust into the hollow of a tree, and thence, as it seemed to him, conveyed into a deep subterranean cave.[59]

To enter league with Herne, to become part of his retinue, is not something to be taken lightly, for "He who has once closed hands with Herne the hunter cannot retreat."[60] The connection between Herne and his bondsmen is eternal and is sealed with a gloriously gothic and sinister flourish: "a wild, demonical laugh, echoed by a chorus of voices, proclaimed [Wyat] in the power of Herne the hunter."[61]

The reason Herne becomes such a demonic, vengeful figure is to do with his genesis. Interestingly, Ainsworth does not offer a single version of Herne's history but many different accounts are given by his characters which the reader must choose between. Even when an expansive, seemingly authoritative version is given, it is immediately undermined. By the end of the novel, one of these versions is shown to be true, yet it is not the one which has become part of the popular imagination.

The first version of the story that we get has echoes of the version of the tale related by Samuel Ireland, fifty years prior to the writing of the novel:

> I know nothing more than that he was a keeper in the forest, who, having committed some heinous crime, hanged himself from a branch of the oak ... which still bears his name ... For this unrighteous act, he cannot obtain rest, but is condemned to wander through the forests at midnight, where he wreaks his vengeance in blasting the trees.[62]

This version of Herne's history suits the early part of the novel, following on, as it does, from the Shakespearean presentation of Herne given in Chapter 1. However, it is immediately challenged by a very different explanation for which there is no antecedence: '"The legend I have heard differs from yours,"' observed the Duke of Richmond. "It runs that the spirit by which the forest is haunted is a wood-demon, who assumes the shape of a ghostly hunter, and seeks to tempt or terrify the keepers to sell their souls to him."'[63] This version of Herne's story, of him being a wood-demon, a natural spirit, seemingly comes from nowhere and is likely a creation of Ainsworth.

The fact that new and different pieces of information are given at different stages of the novel could be down to the way in which it was written.

> An Ainsworth romance came out week by week, in the manner of a soap opera, published as episodes in his own magazine [and later compiled into a single novel]. Every new chapter introduces some fresh character to be woven in the plot, or invents some new twist for an existing one... The attentive reader will catch Ainsworth doing his research as he goes along.[64]

This way of writing likely accounts for the way Herne's history is given much fuller exploration in later parts of the novel.

It is King Henry who first gives the reader the historical time frame from which Herne's tale descends: '"he must be more than a century and a half old, unless the legend is false, he flourished in the time of my predecessor, Richard the Second."'[65] The importance of this line cannot be overstated because, again, there is no antecedence for this information before it appears in Ainsworth's novel and yet it now appears in various works on Herne as a historical fact. For example, Hortus St Michael, in his essay on Herne the Hunter states "The tragedy of Herne played out in the reign of Richard II, twenty-three years full of strife, ruled over by a young king who some say was badly advised."[66]

Here, a critical historical perspective is mixed with a tale which is considered folkloric but is more likely to be literary. There is no indication of where Ainsworth got his information about Herne being from the time of Richard II. There is no other text from 1842 or earlier which contains this information. Again, it could be a piece of oral history but, if so, we know it varies significantly from Ireland's account, which states that Herne's story dates from the reign of Elizabeth I. Similarly, it differs from Halliwell-Phillipps' research, published in the same year as *Windsor Castle,* suggesting Herne's story dates from the reign of Henry VIII. It is Ainsworth who has secured the connection between Herne and Richard II in the public imagination. While *Windsor Castle* could, possibly, be considered a historical novel, it plays fast and loose with historical fact, drawing well-known names into a sensational gothic fantasy. If there is a historical grounding for Herne's story, Ainsworth certainly does not tell us where he found it, even in Book Three which reflects upon *The History of the Castle.*

It is later, in Book Four, Chapter 6, which is called *The Legend of Herne the Hunter,* that Ainsworth gives a full account of Herne's story. Again, he places Herne's story "about the middle of the reign of Richard the Second."[67] Herne was a young keeper of the royal forest, one who was far superior to the other keepers "and consequently in great favour with the king."[68] This meant he was "hated by his comrades, and they concerted together to ruin him."[69] While out hunting one day, the prey, a large stag, charged at the King with its antlers down. Herne threw himself between the two and saved the King's life, being mortally wounded in the process. As Herne lay dying "a tall dark man, in a strange garb, and mounted on a black, wild-looking steed"[70] called Philip Urswick appeared to the King and offered to heal Herne. King Richard agreed. In a bizarre healing ritual, Urswick '"cut off the head of the hart close to the point where the neck joins the skull"[71] saying '"This must be bound on the head of the wounded man."'[72] Urswick kept the injured man at his lodgings for a month, all the time with the stag's head and antlers bound to Herne's brow. Hearing the other keepers' dislike of Herne, Urswick told them: '"I must keep faith with the king. Herne will recover, but he will lose all his skill as an archer – all his craft as a hunter."'[73]

Herne did recover, as promised, and was appointed as King Richard's chief keeper. Richard hung "a chain of gold round his neck."[74] Herne, however, had indeed lost his skills. He was thrown from his horse, was unable to shoot a bow and "had completely lost his mastery over hound and horse."[75] In pure desperation, Herne strode off into the forest and returned with "the links of a rusty chain which he had plucked from a gibbet."[76] "An hour after this, a pedlar, who was crossing the park from Datchet, found him suspended by a rope from a branch of an oak-tree"[77] with antlers bound to his head. This was the tree that subsequently became known as Herne's Oak. The pedlar ran off to get help from the castle, but, when the party returned, "the body was gone; and all that proclaimed it had been there was gone."[78] Later that night "a terrible thunder-storm occurred ... and during its continuance, the oak on which Herne had hanged himself was blasted."[79] The keepers who had robbed Herne of his skills found themselves bound under the same curse that lay on Herne and went back to Herne's Oak to try and break the magic. There they found Urswick, who told them he required them "to form a band for Herne the Hunter, and to serve him as leader"[80] which they do without much persuasion. Here again it is confirmed that Herne's hunters are not spirits but are living men, who "adopted strange disguises."[81] "Night after night, they thus went forth, thinning the herds of deer, and committing other outrages and deprivations."[82] King Richard rode out to discover who was committing such terrible deeds and why. He found Herne underneath his oak tree, who explained that the atrocities were committed '"Because I desire vengeance."'[83] Herne related what the other keepers had done to him and Richard hanged all the guilty keepers from Herne's Oak as punishment. Herne disappeared and was not seen again until the rule of Henry IV, when he led a new band to hunt deer.

It is this story, or variants of it, which have become the basis for Herne's folklore. This is strange as, within the novel, this story is quickly contradicted and by a figure considered by the characters to be Herne himself:

> '"It is true that Herne was a keeper in the reign of Richard the Second ... It is true that he was an expert in all matters of woodcraft, and that he was in high favour with the king; but he was bewitched by a lovely damsel, and not by a weird forester. He carried off a nun and dwelt with her in a cave in the forest, where he assembled his brother keepers, and treated them to the king's venison and the king's wine."'[84]

The stranger goes on to explain that '"...it was through [the nun] that the fiend tempted [Herne]. The charms that proved his undoing were fatal to her also, for in a fit of jealousy he slew her. The remorse occasioned by this deed made him destroy himself."'[85]

This account treats Herne's genesis as a romantic tragedy and not the consequence of a pact made between the jealous keepers and the suspiciously supernatural Urswick. The listeners to this tale are puzzled and point out a big problem with this version – it gives no explanation about why Herne has antlers, although they do wonder if it was linked to him being cuckolded.

Just a few chapters later, we hear from Herne himself that this version story is, in fact, the truth and he had been the mysterious stranger who had corrected those telling the tale about Urswick's curse. Herne explains:

> '"To gain her of whom I have just spoken, and who was already vowed to Heaven, I invoked the powers of darkness. I proffered my soul to the Evil One if he would secure her to me; and the condition demanded by him was that I should become what I am – the fiend of the forest with the power to terrify and to tempt, and with other more fearful and fatal powers besides... She I loved became mine. But she was speedily snatched from me by death, and since then I have known no human passion except hatred and revenge. I have dwelt in this forest, sometimes alone, sometimes at the head of a numerous band, but always exerting a baneful influence."'[86]

So, of all the versions of Herne's genesis presented to us in the novel, Ainsworth definitively endorses one, the love story, as the authentic tale. And yet it is not the one that has been collectively adopted or discussed often in subsequent works on Herne, with a few exceptions. That is possibly because this story, with all its forbidden passions, is more of a plot device. Herne finds himself in love in *Windsor Castle,* and it does not end well.

The object of Herne's affection is Mabel Lyndwood, a demure and pure rustic virgin, one who is visually identical to the nun with whom Herne had previously fallen in love. Herne hunts her down and keeps her in his cave. '"I am chained here by bonds I cannot break."' Mabel emotes, '"Herne has declared that any attempt to escape on my part shall be followed by the death of my grandsire."'[87] While the prospect of being married to Herne repulses Mabel, Herne sees the pair in the light of another legendary Sylvanian couple: '"You shudder, but wherefore? It is a glorious destiny to be the bride of the wild hunter – the fiend who rules the forest, and who in his broad domain is more powerful than the king. Robin Hood had his maid Marian; and what was he compared to me?"'[88]

On the eve of their wedding, Mabel is rescued from the cave by Sir Thomas Wyat and Herne gallops out to reclaim her. Carrying her back to his subterranean kingdom on his horse, a frantic chase ensure. During the chaos, Mabel drowns in lake, her lifeless body carried out by her beloved grandfather, bringing tears to the eyes of the horrified onlookers and readers.

While all of this sounds far too sensational for audiences of the twenty-first century, *Windsor Castle* was phenomenally successful at the time:

> Despite the somewhat hasty composition, Windsor Castle as another great success, its popularity keeping it in print in England (along with *Old St Paul's*), until the late 1960s. In its own day, a French translation appeared daily in *Le Messenger* and a play inspired by the romance, entitled *Herne the Hunter*, did the rounds in London.[89]

While I have not been able to track down a copy of the play, it's hard not to agree with Carver's comment that "As the writers of the play *Herne the Hunter* understood, the horned god is the most interesting character in the novel."[90]

Ainsworth's Herne is a thoroughly engaging character, although not one with as much depth as the other great gothic villains from the nineteenth century, Dracula, and Frankenstein's Creature. Nevertheless, it is easy for us to underestimate the effect that Ainsworth's portrayal has had on shaping our collective image of Herne. He uses details from Shakespeare's play, preserved and augmented by Ireland, adapts the theoretical work of Grimm ("even the white owl which appears initially as Herne's companion was taken from Grimm's account of Tooting Ursula"[91]) and binds it together with his own invention to create a character which resonated in his own time: and in ours. Whether we have heard or him or not, whether we have heard of his novel or not, Ainsworth reshaped

Herne for his readers and we accept many of his literary devices as fact: "True, [Ainsworth's] novels are not great literature, but they commanded massive audiences in the 1830s and 1840s and had a vast influence on popular and literary narratives, both in fiction and more importantly in legend."[92]

Ainsworth's influence can be seen in the ongoing fascination with Herne the Hunter in the nineteenth century. After the felling of the Maiden Oak in 1863, a third tree was planted and named as Herne's Oak, showing the ongoing need to have a national focal point to honour this self-proclaimed "lord of the forest."[93] When that oak blew down in 1906 "Edward VIII had a new Herne's Oak planted on the original site."[94] Just as each century needed a new Herne's Oak, so the people of those centuries created different versions of Herne to walk beneath its branches. While the pious Victorians, filled to the brim with Christian zeal, may have thrilled at the infernal exploits of the demon-hunter, the decline of organised religion in the twentieth century would see Herne step out of the plumes of sulphurous smoke and fully assume the mantle of a god first suggested by Jacob Grimm.

Chapter 4

Carpenter's Shaman

The Lord of the Trees by Hannah Willow

In 1973, Herne the Hunter leaped from the pages of a gloriously eerie[1] children's novel and bewitched a whole new generation of readers. Susan Cooper's astonishing novel, *The Dark is Rising*, tells the story of Will Stanton, who finds himself in a battle between the powers of Light and Dark. And, while Cooper's novel is contemporary, her depiction of Herne owes something to the works of William Harrison Ainsworth and Jacob Grimm.

Cooper's Herne is very firmly located in the grounds of Windsor Great Park:

> Lightning flickered again round them, and the sky roared. Merriman said beside his ear: 'Do you know Herne's Oak?'

'Yes, of course,' Will said at once. He had known the local legend all his life. 'Is that where we are? The big oak tree in the Great Park where – '

He swallowed. How could he not have thought of it? Why had Gramarye taught him everything but this? He went on, slowly, '-where Herne the Hunter is supposed to ride on the eve of Twelfth Night?' Then he looked round fearfully at Merriman. 'Herne?'

'*I go to gather the Hunt,*' Old George had said.

Merriman said, 'Of course. Tonight the Hunt rides."[2]

Notice the thunder and lightning which precedes Herne's appearance, just as in *Windsor Castle,* and that he leads a version of the Wild Hunt. Herne's role as leader of the Hunt is not simply an aspect of his character but is essential to the resolution of the plot: "'The Dark is vanquished, at last, in this encounter. Nothing may outface the Wild Hunt. And Herne and his hounds hunt their quarry as far as they may, to the very ends of the earth.'"[3]

While Cooper's novel helped to cement the connection between Herne and the Wild Hunt, she brings some interesting innovations to her depiction of him, following earlier traditions rather than Ainsworth's novel. This can be seen in Herne's horse and hounds. Rather than his steed being black, as in *Windsor Castle,* "Herne the Hunter wheeled round on a great white horse."[4] Ainsworth's black hounds are replaced with dogs which "were huge white animals, ghostly in the half-light ... Their ears were red, their eyes were red; they were ugly creatures."[5] While the reason for this change in colour reflects the symbolic use of light and dark in the novel – Herne works for the forces of Light, meaning his horse and hounds have to be white – the fact that the hounds are white and have red ears links them to the hunting hounds of Arawn, the king of Annwfn, or the otherworld, as found in the First Branch of *The Mabinogi;*

"the whiteness of the dogs shone so did the redness of their ears."[6] Not only does this connect him to Arawn, who is one of the leaders of the Wild Hunt in Wales, but, as Sioned Davies explains, "red and white are colour traditionally associated with the supernatural in Welsh and Irish tradition."[7]

The other big innovation that Cooper brings is around Herne's appearance, which is far more animalistic than any previous depiction. Herne's arrival in the novel is foreshadowed by a surprising present which Will receives from his brother Stephen on Christmas morning: "'It's a West Indian carnival head. It's old. It's special. Stephen found it in Jamaica.'"[8] Stephen had been given the carnival head by "a very impressive old man"[9] who told him that his younger brother "'will know what to do with it in due course...'"[10] The description of the carnival head is startling:

> The head from which the branching antlers sprang was shaped like the head of a stag, but the ears beside the horns were those of a dog or a wolf. And the face beneath the horns was a human face – but with the round feather-edged eyes of a bird. There was a strong straight human nose, a firm human mouth, set in a slight smile. There was not much else that was purely human about the thing at all. The chin was bearded, but the beard so shaped that it might as easily have been the chin of a goat or deer as a man. The face could have been frightening ... But Will felt that its effect would depend on who was looking at it ... It was a thing made to call out deep responses from the mind. It was very much a thing of the Old Ones.[11]

Of course, when the mask first appears in the novel, the reader has yet to meet Herne the Hunter so does not make the connection between the two. The description, however, is haunting and profound, staying with the reader until the final chapters.

When Herne first appears in the novel beneath the branches of his oak, he is little more than "a shadow ... the size of a man... The creature who owned that shadow was of immense power; Will flinched before the sense of it."[12] Will presents the carnival head to the shadow but it seemingly transforms into Herne's actual head: "he dragged his gaze aside to look properly at the head, the great horned mask that he had given the Hunter to put on. But the head was real."[13] Most noticeable are the eyes, which Cooper returns to frequently: "The golden eyes blinked, feather-fringed and round, with the deliberate blink of an owl's strong eyelids."[14] Again we are taken back to Ainsworth, and to Grimm, but rather than the owl being a companion of Herne, it has now seemingly become part of his physiology:

> The yellow eyes looked at Will again, but they did not see him now; they had grown cold, abstracted, a chill fire mounting in them that brought the cruel lines back to the face. But Will saw the cruelty now as the fierce inevitability of nature. It was not from malice that the Light and servants of the Light would ever hound the Dark, but from the nature of things.[15]

Cooper's Herne is deeply connected to the natural world and the nature of the world. He is so much more than a demonic figure prowling the battlements of Windsor Castle. Cooper's Herne is a localised elemental force. And yet, the fact that Cooper keeps Herne connected to his oak and Windsor Great Park makes her interpretation somewhat of an oddity in the twentieth century because, by 1973, the date of the book's publication, Herne had been acclaimed as a deity for the best part of fifty years.

We are now at another one of those significant moments in the story of Herne. One of those turning points rather like Grimm's naming of Herne as a possible deity and leader of the Wild Hunt back in 1835. And, rather like Grimm's claim, this idea would be picked up by popular culture and disseminated as a truth.

Alongside his appearance in fiction, Herne was a character of interest to the growing neo-pagan movement. In 1929, T. Lowe Thompson published *The History of the Devil: The Horned God of the West*. The book aims to explore the beliefs of "Stone Age Men 9000 years ago"[16] and opens with a plate, a picture depicting "THE MAGICIAN OF THE OLD STONE AGE. A masked man wearing horns of a stag and a horse's tail, drawn at least 9,000 years ago in the Caverne des Trois Frères, Ariège, France"[17]. The cave painting Thompson shows is also known as the Sorcerer. The illustration in his book is not of the original cave art but is based on a version of the cave painting by Henri Breuil, who believed that the picture showed a shamanic figure wearing horns. Whether it is a painting of a shaman or whether it does have horns are both now contested, with general agreement that Breuil's drawing is not an accurate representation of what is on the cave wall. Thompson, however, like others of his time accepted Breuil's claims as fact. Thompson was very much of his time and we need to consider him as such. For example, when discussing which types of people would have been the shamans or magicians in early societies, Thompson writes about gender and sexuality in a way which is now considered to be very outdated, suggesting that the role likely belonged to a certain "feminine type of male ... But not all feminine males. Extreme cases ... would probably have been drowned by any self-respecting tribe ... and pusillanimous, weak-kneed examples are usually reduced to the status of slaves."[18]

Statements such as these may give us pause, and indicate that we should be wary of other content in the book, freighted as it is by Thompson's own prejudices and willingness to interpret his evidence subjectively. In the chapter *Herne and his Kin*, Thompson claims that:

> ...from the dawn of our history and into the fifteenth century there was a powerful and widely spread religion which had survived from very early days; and at times even gained ground as a reaction against the more repressive and inhumane forms of Christianity. We must, therefore, be prepared to give some credence to certain popular tales, which, though adorned by their tellers, none the less had, or could have had, their basis in solid fact. [19]

Thompson establishes two traditions here – Christianity and Witchcraft. He relates a number of popular tales about various "local devil[s]"[20] all of whom are connected to the Wild Hunt. Then he connects them to Herne:

> We would suggest that in this mythical wanderer Herla we may probably see the prototype and original of another kindred being, not less mysterious, who has proved a complete puzzle to folklorists, Shakespeare's Herne the Hunter, who is introduced in the Merry Wives of Windsor (Act iv., sc 4) as well known in ancient tradition...[21]

Thompson here overlooks the fact that in Shakespeare's play Herne is not a "wanderer" but is instead a spirit that is bound to a single tree. His exploits roaming the countryside as leader of the Wild Hunt only date to Grimm's *Deutsch Mythologie* and Ainsworth's *Windsor Castle*, about a century before Thompson was writing.

Thompson goes further to try and secure the link between Herne and ancient deities, turning to the processes by which language changes over time to connect him to the figure of Cernunnos:

> As the Latin *cornu* changes into *horn*, so *Cerne* might change to *Herne*. In any case, the reader may also be

> prepared to recognise Cernunnos and the older magician, who now emerge as the Wild Huntsmen. My assumption that these two forms have been derived from the same palæolitic ancestor and can, indeed be regarded as two aspects of one central figure, will help us to understand the identification of Herlechin and Herne, whom I will take as the most familiar example of the huntsman.[22]

I will come back to Thompson's creative consideration of morphology shortly, but once Thompson has created the link between Herne and Cernunnos, he traces it through both Christianity and popular folklore, or "old wives' tales,"[23] which:

> ... at first confuse our view, but then fall into place to outline the old magician Cernunnos ... Then, as Christianity spreads to the wildest lands, Cernunnos, otherwise Herlechin, as god of the dead, becomes more definitely merged into some devil in the Christian Purgatory, and the magic huntsman stands clear again as Herne, that apparition of a dead keeper to Christian folk, the Windsor witch god to his devotees.[24]

Thompson's claims about how Herne could possibly have been connected to Cernunnos are astonishing, but, at the time, were accepted at face value and began to spread. Just two years later, in 1931, Margaret Murray published her hugely influential book *The God of the Witches*, a history of "the Old Religion"[25] which went on to influence the development of modern neo-paganism. She, like Thompson, used the cave painting of the Sorcerer as her starting point, before tracing the tradition of the horned god, including Cernunnos, through time. Turning to Britain, she wrote that:

> The first recorded instance of the continuation of the worship of the Horned God in Britain is in 1303, when the Bishop of

> Coventry was accused before the Pope of doing homage to the devil in the form of a sheep. The fact that a man in so high a position as a bishop could be accused of practicing the Old Religion shows that the cult of the Horned God was far from being dead and was in all probability still the chief worship of the bulk of the people[26]

Shortly after, Murray brings Herne into the conversation, although her consideration of him and his folklore is problematic:

> Herne the Hunter, with horns on his head, was seen in Windsor Forest by the Earl of Surrey in the reign of Henry VIII, and after that period it was a favourite accusation against all political enemies that they were in league with 'the foul fiend' who appeared to them in human form horned like a bull or a stag.[27]

The issue with Murray's account is that it based on a story which is simply is not true. What she recounts is the plot of *Windsor Castle,* a work of fiction, and not any kind of recorded historical fact.

Both Thompson's and Murray's inclusion of Herne the Hunter in their works on horned gods are flawed. For one thing, they both take as their starting point a cave painting of a horned shaman which probably did not have horns at all. Thompson's link between the names of Herne and Cernunnos may, on the surface, seem to be convincing (the Latin word *cornu* does, indeed, mean horn, just as Thompson claimed), but is far from secure. Remember, we have already seen in Chapter 2 that the word heron is one possible root for the word Herne. Jeremy Harte goes further, noting:

> ... nine other versions of the name Herne have been proposed by recent authors, many prepared to advance

> multiple interpretations without pausing to reflect that if any one of these is right the others are likely to be wrong. Among profuse references to Cornwall, Cerne Abbas, herons and hoarstones it is possible, eventually, to discover that Herne is a common mediaeval surname.[28]

Using online etymological dictionaries give a range of roots for the name Herne, but none of them link to words which are remotely close to Cernunnos. And we must not forget about poor old Rychard Horne, discovered by Halliwell-Phillipps as a possible source for Herne. If Herne's folklore is traceable to him then, surely, he cannot be Cernunnos too?

That is not to say that Thompson and Murray's arguments are not compelling, particularly in the way that Thompson explores the idea of ancient magicians or shamans with horned headdresses. The copies of the cave painting in the Caverne des Trois Frères may not be accurate but we know that antlers have been worn and used in shamanic practice for centuries. In Britain, the Mesolithic site of Star Carr in Yorkshire is notable for a number of headdresses or antler frontlets found at the site. I was lucky enough to visit an exhibition of these artefacts in Yorkshire Museum during the writing of this book and they really are astonishing and incredibly moving to see.

> They were usually made from red deer skulls, though a roe deer skull was found ... To make them, people removed parts of the skull, including the nose, jaw and brain of the deer ... Some of the headdresses have holes drilled into them and it is thought that these might have helped in fastening the headdresses to the head.[29]

As well as being found at Star Carr, headdresses such of these have been used by Siberian Shamans.

While this may be true, the fact that Shamans are known to wear antlered headdresses does not mean that the figure of Herne is linked to such practices. As we have already seen, wearing horns on one's head in Shakespeare's time had a very different meaning, and it is from that time that our evidence for Herne begins. "Herne has to be understood in his context" argues Harte "... comparison with the antlers of Star Carr, Neolithic Bulgaria and the Tungus tribesmen will not shed any further light on the matter."[30] That is not to say that we need to completely discount the work of Thompson and Murray. After all it went on to have significant influence on popular culture and the development of neo-Paganism. We just need to be a little wary of stating the connection between Herne and Cernunnos as absolute when there are so many different sources from which his folklore could have sprung. So far in this journey we have seen him being framed as a wood spirit, a demon, the ghost of a historically identifiable individual, a theatrical invention, and a story to frighten children as well as leader of the Wild Hunt and horned God. It is also worth reflecting at this stage that the figure of Cernunnos themselves is "oddly elusive,"[31] only being mentioned in a single inscription in France, with the name being subsequently applied to a range of images of horned deities across the European continent.

By way of a warning about blindly following the seemingly secure connections which surround newly revealed deities, I want to briefly consider another God who was anointed in the early twentieth century but has now disappeared from the English pantheon. That is the God Cole, "corresponding to that ancient Irish fertility god of the great pit, the Dagda, in England seems to be Celi or Coeli ... the Concealed One, the piping god, probably the oldest traceable deity in England."[32] While Cole was not an identifiable folkloric figure like Herne, there was some significant creative and academic work around him in the twentieth century which has now been disproved. Ross Nichols, the founder of modern Druidry, gave a lecture entitled *Cole of the Chilterns* where he pulled together evidence to prove the deity was remembered in place names such as Colchester and figures such as Cerne Abbas. Poet Laureate John Masefield wrote an extended poem called *King Cole,* in which a much beloved King:

...reached the judging-place
(There where the scales are even, the sword keen),
The Acquitting Judges granted him a grace,
Aught he might choose, red, black, from king to ace,
Beneath the bright arch of the heaven's span;
He chose, to wander earth, the friend of man.[33]

In short, Cole became supernatural god-like figure who wandered the highways of the Chiltern Hills who, in Masefield's poem, helped a bunch of travelling show people to succeed with their performance. However, the whole idea of a God called Cole has been discredited, and even the some of the tales of a mortal, historical King Cole are seen by some as "a flight of fancy."[34]

As well as writing a poem about King Cole, Masefield also included a version of him in his much-loved 1935 children's book *The Box of Delights*. The character of Cole Hawlings, although ultimately revealed in the book to be the medieval philosopher Ramon Lully, is clearly meant to be the beneficent deity, Cole, even down to the fact that he is a travelling showman. More importantly for us, he shares the narrative with an incarnation of Herne the Hunter which is the first to be directly informed by the work of Thompson and Murray.

The Box of Delights is a book that is well-loved and versions of it continue to enchant audiences into the twenty-first century. It tells the story of Kay Harker, a privileged yet orphaned 1930s schoolboy, home from boarding school for Christmas. Just like Will Stanton in *The Dark is Rising*, Kay finds himself trapped in a battle between the forces of light and darkness. "Now that the Wolves are Running, as you will have seen, perhaps you would do something to stop their Bite?"[35] Cole Hawlings asks him, shortly before entrusting Kay with the Box, a magical artefact which he must keep from falling into the wrong hands. To help him, Kay has an array of magical helpers, and Herne the Hunter is one of them.

Kay first encounters Herne in Chapter 2, although he is in disguise:

> From the cross-roads behind him a rider came cloppetting up, the horse slipping a little, the rider bent into a long white overall to keep the snow from blowing down his neck ... Kay did not recognise the man, but he noticed that his eyes were very bright...
>
> 'They tell me, Master Harker,' the man said, 'that Wolves are Running. If you see Someone,' he added meaningly, 'say Someone's safe.'
>
> 'I will,' Kay said.
>
> 'And, look out for fun, Master Harker,' the man said, shaking up the horse and riding on. Kay watched him go. He went skittering a little sideways and champing on the bit. It seemed to Kay that the man's arms were hung with little silver chains which jangled. Later it seemed to him that it was not a horse and rider at all, but a great stag from the forest. Certainly the figure that passed round the bend out of sight was a stag.[36]

Herne's ability to shapeshift into a stag is not something that we have seen in print since the 1602 quarto of *Merry Wives*. It should also be noted that Herne has become completely detached from Windsor. Masefield's story is set in the fictional areas of Condicote and Tatchester (there is a hint from the poem

King Cole that Condicote may be in the Chilterns but that is not specified in the novel.)[37]

Kay meets Herne more fully when he opens the Box itself, in a scene which has become central in every version of the novel produced on TV and stage. In the novel, Kay opens the Box and hears a multitude of birds singing. Soon he feels as if he is "staring into the opening of a wood."[38] Trees dapple the light and an array of animals and insects roister around the glade. "While he gazed into the heart of summer and listened to the murmur and the singing, he heard another noise like the tinkling of little bells... He remembered the strange rider who has passed him in the street the day before."[39] It is then that Kay and the reader properly meets Herne:

> At first he thought that the figure was one of those giant red deer, long since extinct: it bore enormous antlers. Then he saw that it was a great man, antlered at the brow, dressed in deerskins and moving with the silent slow grace of a stag; and, although he was so like a stag, he was hung about with little silver chains and bells.
>
> Kay knew at once that this was Herne the Hunter, of whom he had often heard. 'Ha, Kay,' Herne the Hunter said, 'are you coming into my wild wood?'[40]

Masefield's Herne is not a human, although he takes human form. He is a spirit, possibly a god, who is deeply connected to the forest and can take the shape of a stag. Kay, worried that he shall "'never know a hundredth part of all the things there are to know,'"[41] accepts Herne's offer to "'be a stag with me in the wild wood.'"[42]

What follows is an extended episode where Kay and Herne transform from stags to wild duck to fish. It is a scene which strongly evokes Taliesin's transformations while being chased by Cerridwen. The idea of transformation into animals as a way of teaching and learning would be seen again in T.H. White's *The Once and Future King*, the first part of which was published just a few years after *The Box of Delights* in 1938. Masefield writes:

> While Kay was enjoying the water Herne asked, 'Did you see the wolves in the wood?'
> 'No,' Kay said.
> 'Well, they were there,' Herne said; 'and that was why I moved. Did you see the hawks in the air?'
> 'No,' Kay said.
> 'Well, they were there,' Herne said; 'and that was why I plunged. And do you see the pike in the weeds?'
> 'No,' Kay said.
> 'He is there,' Herne said. 'Look.'[43]

The lesson of looking and seeing what is there is crucial to the novel. The pair turn back to stags and return to the glade to "a great ruined oak tree" before "somehow, the figure of Herne, which had been so stag-like, became like the oak and merged with Herne till Kay could see nothing but the tree. What had been Herne's antlers were now a few old branches and what had seemed silver chains dangling from Herne's wrists were now the leaves rustling."[44] Masefield's Herne does not live in or beneath an oak tree, he physically becomes the oak tree, one which stands in the middle of a forest and not Windsor Great Park. In *The Box of Delights*, Herne no longer inhabits the wood. He is the wood. This is the first time Herne physically changes into a tree, meaning that, for Masefield, Herne's Oak is literally Herne.

Herne returns to the novel when Kay wishes to go back into the past to find Arnold of Todi, the creator of the Box: "In front of [Kay] was what seemed like the bole of a ruined tree, but it was Herne the Hunter, clad in some pelt, powdered with snow."[45] Herne does help Kay to get into the past and helps him return to his own time too: "At this instant he heard himself called: 'Kay! Kay!' There behind him in a little bay of the sea, so bright and beautiful, were two figures whom he saw to be Herne the Hunter and the woman of the oak tree."[46] The Woman of the Oak Tree is another occasional participant in the action and can be considered as a version of the Cailleach, the Goddess to Herne's horned God. They take Kay back across the seas of time on "the most beautiful dolphins."[47]

Herne and the Woman of the Oak Tree appear one final time at the end of the novel, where Kay and his friends are trying to get to Tatchester Cathedral to hold Midnight Mass, the first ceremony of Christmas. Finding themselves stranded in deep snow, they hear the sound sleigh bells. The Lady of the Oak Tree arrives first with "a magnificent teams of harnessed lions drawing a long sled."[48] Close behind is another sled pulled by:

> ... a team of eight of the most beautiful unicorns that ever stepped ... They were driven by a man, whose sleeves were hung with little silver chains...
>
> 'Oh, it is Herne again,' Kay said. 'I do love going with Herne the Hunter.'[49]

What follows is the "most beautiful drive through the heavens"[50] as they fly through the skies to reach the cathedral and save Christmas. This mixing of Christian and Pagan elements may have surprised some readers at the time as Masefield "occasionally turned to Christian themes in his writing."[51] However, the shaping of the characters of Cole, Herne and the Woman of the Oak Tree shows a developed interest in more traditional, British forms of belief, implying that Masefield may well have had his finger on the pulse of works such as those by Thompson and Murray. While there may have been an early Pagan influence on Masefield's life,[52] we cannot consider Masefield to be a pagan author. Cole Hawlings himself addresses this within the novel when he and Kay see a cave painting: 'That was our old religion, Master Harker,' Cole said, nodding towards it 'It was nothing like so good as the new, of course, but it was good fun in its day, though, because it ended in a feast.'[53]

As mentioned, Masefield's novel continues to enchant and there have been two theatrical productions in the twenty-first century. The first was staged at Wilton's Music Hall in London in 2017 and was written by Piers Torday. A revised production, also written by Torday, was staged by the Royal Shakespeare Company in 2023. Torday gives an interesting reason for Herne's connection to the Box. Herne tells the audience: "I am Herne the Hunter. This box is made from my oak and I remain its guardian. Welcome to my wild wood."[54] Herne's big scene is the scene of transformation, where he and Kay become different animals. However, in the play, these lessons are shared with Kay's friends, with Kay becoming the stag, Maria the duck and Peter the fish. But perhaps more significantly, Herne takes the audience, and Kay back in time to "Christmas Eve, six years ago"[55] so that we see how and why Kay was orphaned. This is not a topic that Masefield goes near, focusing instead on a rollicking good adventure. The scene has echoes of the episode in the novel where Herne tells Kay to pay more attention. We learn that Kay's parents perished in a fire:

Herne The Box allows you to travel through time, Master Kay, but you cannot change it.

Kay Then what is the point? Why did you show me again? Did you think I had forgotten? When I think about that moment every single day?

Herne No, Kay, I wanted you to look. You weren't looking.

Kay What am I looking for?

Herne The truth, Kay.[56]

In the adapted version staged by the Royal Shakespeare Company, the character of Herne was played by a female actor. The casting choice neatly ties together two of Masefield's characters, with Herne stating "I am Herne the Hunter, the Lady of the Oak."[57]

However, perhaps the most well-known adaptation of *The Box of Delights* is the 1984 BBC Television series, which was shown on BBC1 weekly from 21st November, with the final episode shown on Christmas Eve. Herne the Hunter was played by Glynn Baker who reflected on the role in the documentary *Time and Tide: The Making of the Box of Delights*, available on the 40th anniversary BluRay of the series. Baker noted that "[Herne] isn't actually a very big part in it. He just appears at star moments!" Baker has a point here. Herne is not in the book or TV series very much at all but does make a significant impact whenever he appears.

Herne appears several times in the series: "He is one character but he appears in five or six or seven different guises" Baker reflects. Indeed, Herne does appear numerous times, although he often assumes the roles of minor characters in the novel. He first appears dressed in his full Herne outfit in episode two. Baker makes a striking figure with his angular jaw and thick mane of hair. He is dressed simply in trousers and a jerkin, with a swathe of black fur wrapped around him. On his head is a deer's skull with two good sized antlers. He is a very elemental, 'down-to-earth' figure. There is nothing scary about him at all. When Kay is planning to go into the past, Herne grips his shoulders and smiles at him, full of admiration for the boy. In the final episode, Kay even refers to Herne as his 'friend.'

It is worth noting that all of Herne's key scenes in the series take place on animated or obviously fake backgrounds. This was done deliberately, with director Renny Rye reflecting that "Using animation was a decision I made quite early on ... I thought it was a way of showing the difference when Kay went into a complete fantasy world." The scene where Kay first joins Herne in his wild wood, called 'Herne's Forest' in the script, is a wonderfully evocative short piece of animation. Like the figure of Herne himself, it does not take up much time within the episode but was one of the key scenes which stuck with viewers of the show. There is a focus on the eyes of the stag, the duck and the fish throughout the animation, with the sequence finishing on the eyes of a young stag, Kay, as Herne transforms into an oak tree. This is key in helping develop the idea that Herne helps Kay to see things more clearly.

I saw the series when it was first screened in 1984 and re-watch the series every year. By far my favourite sequence is in the sixth episode, set on Christmas Eve. Herne and the Woman of the Oak Tree, named in the series as the Old Lady, sweep in across the snow-covered landscape in their sleighs to collect Kay and his friends from a snow drift. "Herne the Hunter!" the Old Lady exclaims "Keep your Lions away from my Unicorns!" It is an interesting swap from Masefield's novel, where Herne has the team of unicorns and the Woman the lions. It makes sense Herne has the unicorns, after all, he also has horns. Maybe they were swapped because lions sit more comfortably with the masculine aspect of traditional gender roles. However, it is covered in the series by Herne having a magnificent mane of hair so that he looks ever so slightly leonine. As the sleighs set off through the skies towards Tatchester cathedral, we see the lights of the houses far below, frozen in a snowy landscape. And then, by way of homage to that familiar trope of Father Christmas riding his sleigh on Christmas Eve, first the sleigh pulled by unicorns, then the sleigh pulled by lions, dance across the Moon. Christmas has been saved by the Old Gods. Herne the Hunter has saved the day. Let the festivities commence!

The TV adaptation of *The Box of Delights* was a huge success, nominated for five BAFTAs and winning three. But Christmas was not the only time Herne the Hunter was on television in

1984. In fact, he was an integral part of the biggest tea-time series of the decade, which would give us what many still consider to be the defining twentieth century image of Herne.

Shown in the peak Saturday tea-time slot on ITV television between 1984 and 1986, *Robin of Sherwood* was a landmark piece of television that shaped a generation's approach to the legendary characters of Sherwood Forest and Herne the Hunter. In the show, Herne was totally dislocated from Windsor Great Park and became a resident of Sherwood. Whereas Masefield had softened that dislocation by largely tying Herne's appearances to the Box, Richard 'Kip' Carpenter, the creator and writer of *Robin of Sherwood*, did no such thing. There is no explanation as to why he is in Sherwood rather than Windsor. He just is.

What is also unique about Carpenter's Herne is that he is human. He is not a spirit or a ghost haunting a tree, he is not a demon accompanied by thunder and lightning. Herne, played by actor John Abineri, is flesh and blood, although he has very potent magical powers. In the documentary *Nothing is Forgotten*, available on the *Complete Robin of Sherwood* BluRray, Carpenter reflects that the character was "a kind of semi-supernatural Merlin figure that I created as a sort of mentor, guide, speaker in riddles." Carpenter evokes the figure of the shaman in his Herne, who can commune directly with the gods.

In the very first episode of the series, called *Robin Hood and the Sorcerer*, Robin of Loxley, played by Michael Praed, encounters Herne in Sherwood Forest. Herne, dressed in his iconic shamanic robes, with an entire stag's head perched atop his own, asks Robin "Do you fear me?" to which Loxley replies "Why should I fear you? You are just a man." "I am your destiny" Herne replies. There is an echo of this conversation later in the episode when Herne takes Robin to his cave. This time, Robin says, rather more forcefully, "You are no god!" to which Herne replies "We can all be gods. All of us ... When the horned one possesses me, I am Herne the Hunter." So, although the human, shamanic character is referred to throughout the series as Herne, Herne is actually a god, lord of the forest, lord of the trees, who uses the shaman as way of communicating with the human characters.

When reflecting further on the character, Carpenter specifically linked Herne the Hunter to the figure of the horned god as explored in the works of Thompson and Murray: "Herne the Hunter is an old myth, this idea of the forest god, the male god, the male principle." This ties Carpenter's vision of Herne specifically to the work being undertaken in the burgeoning neo-Pagan community in the twentieth century. Just as Grimm's attribution of Herne as a leader of the Wild Hunt was popularised through Ainsworth's novel *Windsor Castle*, so Thompson and Murray's discussions of Herne as an incarnation of the horned god finds its most potent expression in Carpenter's vision. And, just as with Ainsworth's novel, Carpenter used the most popular form of its day, in this case, television, to disseminate that vision to the widest possible audience.

The television series reenchants England's forests, making them a place of magic and wonder:

> The most obvious liberty taken with the tales of the Greenwood was the generous helping of Fantasy and Magic in the series ... Robin Hood is more than just the bold, idealistic, Saxon-blooded folk hero, he's also the spiritually empowered 'son' of Herne the Hunter, Lord of the Trees.
>
> This more fantastic slant upon the legend may seem at odds with the second major departure from the traditional Robin Hood adventures – a move towards greater realism ... Herne occasionally intervened directly (for example to save, on separate occasions, Robin and Marion from lethal crossbow/arrow attacks) and often acted as a warning to the outlaws, thus giving them the upper hand.[58]

While Herne may be the central magical touchstone for the series, magic and occult practices swirl between the trees of Carpenter's Sherwood. The Sorcerer alluded to in the title of the first episode could be Herne but is more likely to be the Count de Belleme, a recurring nemesis of Robin's throughout the first two series. In *The Children of Israel*, the resolution involves the magical powers of the Kabbalah. There are numerous witches, from the predatory Lillith in *The Enchantment* to the pig-obsessed crone, Mad Mabh, in *Rutterkin*. Richard O'Brien plays Gulnar in series three, a dark Druid intent on magically taking over the forest. "The magic and mysticism was ever-present but generally understated, making it appear a regular occurrence of life."[59]

The mystical nature of the series was heightened using music, with the Irish group Clannad providing the sound track. Herne has his own theme, a piece beginning with low sounds which conjure up the swirling mists of the forest, before moving into something more akin to the beating of a shamanic drum. Visually the series makes great use of smoke machines and filters to create a somewhat romantic vision, although one which is grounded within medieval realism. Herne often appears standing in a halo of light and mist, making him seem larger than life and otherworldly. His long cloak, or coat, disguises the shape of his human body while the full stag's head and antlers he wears on his head almost completely distract the audience from the actor's own facial features. While the image of Carpenter's Herne has remained etched in the popular consciousness, it is not one Carpenter particularly liked:

> Here was this guy with a stag's head on, trying to act through what looked like a hatstand. It gave him a very strange and mysterious look ... It was a shame. I'd seen it as a man wearing horns, which is the traditional Herne image, or at least the skull on top of his head of a stag

> with antlers, so we could have the actor, John Abineri, playing Herne, acting Herne. So, to get around this I had him take the damn thing off occasionally so that we could see him without it.

What Carpenter describes as his ideal costume for Herne is closer to the outfit worn by Glynn Baker in *The Box of Delights*. Baker and Abineri play very different versions of Herne. Whereas Baker is younger, a more friendly and accessible figure, Abineri is obviously older than all the other characters in Sherwood, marking him out as the mentor, the Merlin figure for Robin. This was a very deliberate decision on behalf of the production team of *Robin of Sherwood*, who wanted a band of outlaws who were young, idealistic and vaguely contemporary.

Herne appears in most of the episodes of the series (apart from a noticeable run of absences in series 3, where Carpenter shared writing duties with Anthony Horowitz) but there are some key episodes which help drive his character forward.

The first two episodes of season one form a single story, *Robin Hood and the Sorcerer*. These episodes establish the world of the series, introduce the main characters and retell some of the most well-known aspects of the Robin Hood myth, such as his quarterstaff fight with Little John. They also introduce us to Herne and how he will operate within the narrative of the series. For example, as discussed above, it is in this episode that we learn that Herne is a god channelled through a human shaman and that he has a secret cave, to which visitors must travel across water, where much of his magic is done. These episodes also introduce us to some key items in the possession of Herne that will develop across the course of the three series.

The first item of interest is a silver arrow, which is covered by ancient writing and Celtic scroll work. The first episode opens with Robin of Loxley's father, Ailric, being killed by the men of the Sheriff of Nottingham, played by Nicholas Grace.

They take the silver arrow which he has been keeping safe for Herne the Hunter. In the second episode the arrow reappears in the hands of the Sheriff, who tells us that it was "described by Gildas the Monk over five hundred years ago, but it's even older than that. Much older." Later in the same episode he describes it as one of the "secret symbols of England," "A cult object, like a sceptre or a cross. A symbol. An English thing. Magic." When Herne gives Robin an intoxicating drink, he asks Loxley "What binds the hunter to the hunted?" Robin cannot immediately answer but eventually realises that the answer to the riddle is the silver arrow, being offered as a prize by the Sheriff in an archery contest. Robin obviously wins and tries to give the arrow back to Herne who refuses, stating that the arrow is Robin's protection against the forces of evil mustering against him. When the dastardly Count de Belleme, played with relish by Anthony Valentine, takes Marion and insists that an enchanted Robin kills her using Herne's arrow, Robin dupes the wicked sorcerer and instead pierces Belleme's heart with the arrow. The arrow also plays a significant role in bringing Marion back to life in *The King's Fool* and is the centre of the action in *The Enchantment*, where the witch, Lillith, tricks Robin into giving it to her. She uses it to bring de Belleme back to life. De Belleme isolates Robin and fires the arrow at him, stating "Herne's arrow shall kill his son." However, just as the arrow is about to pierce Robin's breast, Herne appears and grabs it, handing it back to Robin, finally defeating de Belleme.

The other significant item Herne gives Robin in the first episode is a sword, "Albion, one of the seven swords of Wayland, charged with the power of light and darkness." The sword connects both Herne and Robin to England and its mythical past. In the second season double episode, *The Swords of Wayland*, a group of devil-worshipping nuns are attempting to gather all seven swords for nefarious purposes. Herne warns Robin: "Hear me and heed me for I am Herne, Lord of the Trees.

They that seek to shatter the bolts that hold back the evil one must first take Albion from you. Hold steadfast. It is written that the servants of Lucifer will find the seventh sword at the village on the rock. Swear to guard it with your heart's blood." At the successful conclusion of the episode, Herne tells Robin that "Nothing we make is good or evil until we use it." Albion, Herne reassures us, "is in good hands." By series three, Robin of Loxley has been killed and the mantle of Robin Hood has been taken over by Robert of Huntingdon, played by Jason Connery. The episode, *The Power of Albion,* tells of how the sword passes to its new master. Herne, in voiceover, reads the words on the sword, stating "Herne's son is my master, I cannot slay him." When Guy of Gisburne, played by Robert Addie, tries to kill Huntingdon with Albion, he is overwhelmed by the spirit of the sword and falls to the ground. Huntingdon assumes the sword as his own. Herne appears to him and his followers commanding them "To help the weak, defend the helpless and fight against tyranny. Robin I'th'hood, so must it be."

There are some key motifs, found in *Robin Hood and the Sorcerer* and other early episodes which help to define Herne and Robin's relationship for the viewers. As mentioned, the naming of Robin Hood as Herne's son occurs in the very first episode, with Loxley warning Gisburne "Herne's Son has claimed his kingdom" at the episode's end. The name is used to delineate Robin throughout all three series, with *Herne's Son* becoming the title of the two-part episode where Huntingdon assumes the role. In *The Witch of Elsdon,* Robin and his friends use the phrase "Herne protect us" before toasting, drinking and eating. Again, this appears throughout the series, helping cement Herne as the central spiritual figure of this landscape, replacing, as it does, the more traditional Christian grace.

In the episode *The King's Fool,* Marion, played by Judy Trott, is fatally wounded by Gisburne. Robin takes her to a nearby stone circle, called Rhiannon's Wheel. There, Robin gives Herne an epithet which has become so deeply associated with him that it is now embedded in the popular imagination. "Herne, Lord of the Trees, I call on you." Herne appears, telling Robin to take out the arrow. He then performs his most significant piece of magic across all three series, seemingly turning the wheel of time backwards, saving Marion and reuniting Robin with his men. "The wheel turns" Herne announces, as the camera spins, dizzily, around the stones. The episode ends with Herne, a god standing on the earth, resplendent in a beam of light between monolithic stones and a louring sky.

There is a contrasting scene in a stone circle at the end of the third series, in the final episode, *The Time of the Wolf*. The malevolent Gulnar creates a copy of Robin out of clay with the specific intention of killing Herne. "The Hunter will become the Hunted" Gulnar gloats. Herne meets the copy of Robin at the Ring of the Nine Maidens, where Herne is wounded and thrown to the ground shortly after arriving. He is no longer the all-powerful god but rather a very human shaman who is somewhat showing his age. Rescued and healed by Robin, Herne's long-term future is uncertain. "There will be no Time of the Wolf" he says. Huntingdon replies "Not yet. But one day there will."

However, it is the fourth episode of season two, called *The Lord of the Trees*, where viewers really get to embrace Carpenter's vision of Herne. The episode is mostly set in the village of Wickham, where the community are celebrating the festival of The Blessing, a rite dedicated to honouring Herne. Herne appears several times to the villagers during the festival and a pact is made between the villagers and Herne, ensuring a successful harvest to come. While the specifics about the festival are somewhat hazy, there is a distinct feel of the neo-Pagan festival of Beltane about the whole thing. There is plenty of music, with villagers coupling up and dancing between two fires. Wickham has an altar to Herne bedecked with antlers and a tree close by which the villagers believe is sacred to him. We are told that this is an ancient festival which has been honoured for hundreds of years and that, during the period of the festival, no blood must be shed. Guy of Gisburne, humorously renamed Guy the Gamekeeper, grumbles that there is an awful lot of poaching that goes on during the festival. In fact, the festival reveals an interesting divide between the different classes in the world of the show: "Herne [is] revered as a god by the commoners and dismissed as superstitious mumbo-jumbo but the nobility, and in particular the Sheriff and Gisburne."[60] When Gisburne attempts to cut down Herne's sacred tree, the Abbot Hugo warns him to "Leave well alone or you may find out these old gods aren't quite as dead as you think." After firing an arrow at Herne, Gisburne ends up being pursued through the forest by his spirit, driving him mad. "Save me!" Gisburne cries, arriving back at the castle, "The forest! The trees!"

Carpenter's vision of Robin Hood and Herne the Hunter remains a compelling one, influencing later retellings of the story and continuing to hold a special place in the popular imagination. The aesthetics of the series resonate strongly with those of modern neo-Paganism and, for many, but not all, it is Carpenter's Herne that will come to mind whenever Herne the Hunter is mentioned. Carpenter took the ideas set out by Thompson and Murray and turned them into television drama. By making the outlaws of Sherwood Forest contemporary and accessible for a large Saturday evening television audience, and by positioning Herne as their guardian, Carpenter secured Herne's position as a deity. "It's pure entertainment," Carpenter reflected about his show. But he was wrong. It was far more beautiful, significant and transformational than that.

Interestingly, the early twentieth century saw many physical sightings of Herne in Windsor, as well as others hearing the Wild Hunt galloping around the area. Whether they belonged to the "retired colonel looking out of the window of his lodgings in [Windsor] Castle in 1915"[61] or "The young guardsman who panicked in 1976 and shot at a statue because he saw it growing horns,"[62] reactions to Herne became as unique as the individual who encountered him. No longer sustained simply by the popularity of Shakespeare and established in the popular imagination by Ainsworth, Herne began to exist on his own terms, as a leader of the Wild Hunt and as an old god, even though the evidence for him actually being either of these is somewhat questionable. Every sighting brought something different to his story. Works like those by Cooper, Masefield and Carpenter gave us contrasting perspectives of him as an elemental, animalistic force, as a child's best friend who helps him see more clearly and as a shaman who could channel an ancient god. These versions of Herne were held in the popular imagination, together, and without contradiction because the way that we perceived Herne depended not on what a single authority told us about him but because we could now pick the version of him we liked the best.

The end of twentieth century saw Herne move beyond the control of any one creator. Instead, he belonged to the children playing in the woods with their friends, imagining they were Robin Hood. He belonged to the visitor of Windsor, hoping to catch sight of his antlers, glinting in the moonlight. He belonged to the people turning their back on established religion and beginning to follow a Pagan path. By the century's end, Herne belonged to all of us. And it is that democratisation of Herne which would shape his path into the twenty-first century

Chapter 5

Gilbert's Starlings

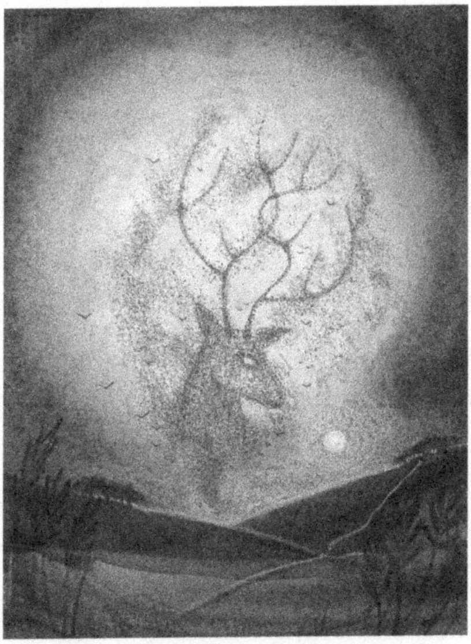

The Murmuration by Hannah Willow

The influence of Richard Carpenter's Herne has lasted well into the twenty-first century. One of the more recent flowerings of this incarnation came in 2024 when a deck of cards called *The Sherwood Oracle* was released. With deeply evocative artwork by Anne Yvonne Gilbert, the deck was created by Mark Ryan, who played Nazir in *Robin of Sherwood*, and well-known writer John Matthews. Alongside the usual Sherwood Forest suspects, such as Robin, Marion and Little John, Ryan and Matthews include Herne the Hunter.

Gilbert's illustration of Herne is gorgeous. Riding through an autumnal forest under a full moon, Herne is closer to Carpenter's original vision for his character, with a stag's skull on his head. Ryan and Matthew's book tells us:

> The association of Herne with Robin Hood goes back a long way. Robin himself is a type of Green Man, an immortally ancient figure who represents the vital power of nature. Though he may seem to belong to other and later traditions, Herne is part of the lore of the wildwood.[1]

For me, there are many issues with this statement, with the first sentence being particularly problematic – the association between Herne and Robin Hood does not go back a particularly long way, unless you count 1984 as a long time ago.

What is also problematic about this section is the linking of Herne, via Robin, to the figure of the Green Man, which Ryan and Matthews claim is "an immortally ancient figure." While the association between Herne and the Green Man is often repeated[2], recent work has cast doubt on just how old the figure of the Green Man is. As one reviewer of Stephen Miller's book *The Green Man in Medieval England* noted, the Green Man "is a distinctly Christian image, rich with interlaced scriptural and traditional symbolism, and he is thoroughly medieval."[3] In other words, not "immortally ancient."

The connection between Herne and the Green Man was explored by John Matthews in his 2001 book *The Quest for the Green Man*. Herne has an entire section in the book, called *The Green Huntsman*. The section begins

> A character who forms an important link between the vegetative, animal, and human aspects of the Green Man is Herne the Hunter. Over the centuries he has assumed the mantle of earlier archetypes, including that of the Norse god Woden, a leader of the Wild Hunt.[4]

What is pleasing here is to see Matthews being clear that Herne's association with the Wild Hunt is a later addition to his mythology, although, as the chapter goes on, Matthews becomes less clear when differentiating between Herne and the archetypes which have been imposed upon him. "References to Herne as leader of the Wild Hunt are found in many cultures throughout the ages"[5] Matthews claims. This statement, presented as fact, is highly misleading. As we have seen, the first reference to Herne as a leader of the Wild Hunt was not until 1835 and although this mention occurred in a German text, Herne was only briefly mentioned by Grimm as a comparative figure. Presentations of Herne are generally only found in English texts, not in other cultures.

Matthews continues:

> In Germany, it is said that an old man named Honest Eckart goes in front of the Hunt, warning people to get out of the way. Eckart is often described, like Woden or Odin, as having a long grey beard and a broad-brimmed hat, and as riding a white horse. In one version of the story he calls out:
>
> *Fly then, quickly, make no stay*
> *For Herne the Hunter rides this way.*[6]

Again, while Matthews is not exactly wrong, this quotation is highly misleading. The rhyme is presented as if it were a version of a traditional tale emanating from Germany. However, it actually comes from the Winter 1983 edition of the magazine *Fantasy Tales*, from a short story called *The Green Man* by Kelvin Jones. Matthews does not credit Jones' story in his book.

Later in the chapter, Matthews states, without any real evidence, that:

> Herne springs from the Saxon tradition, and it is to this cultural milieu that we must look for his origins

> ... Etymologically, the names Woden and Herne are connected. When Woden leads his select band of warriors, the *herjar,* he is given the name Herian, which mutates into Harilo, Hevela, Herlake and Herla – and later on, Herne.[7]

Matthews here repeats the technique used by Thompson in 1929, of attempting to show how names and words have changed to link Herne together with an older deity. However, while we may find this convincing, there is no evidence that this progression is authentic. Just as with Thompson trying to connect Herne and Cernunnos, there are plenty of alternative explanations for the lineage of Herne's name, as we have seen.

When Matthews turns his attention to *The Merry Wives of Windsor,* we find similar issues with his account. "We know that Shakespeare's knowledge of folklore was considerable and that he seldom invents when he can refer to a genuine story."[8] Again, this is not true. Shakespeare was a playwright, not a folklorist, and freely adapted ancient tales so that they suited his dramatic purpose. When considering the differences between the 1602 quarto edition and the 1623 folio version of the play, Matthews proposes it was "altered by an anonymous author who probably lived in the Windsor area ... Whatever story Shakespeare knew it seems likely that the author of these additional lines knew better."[9] As we have seen, this is not true and that the quarto version is considered to be a based on a staged version of the play. To be fair, Matthews does alter this claim in his 2016 book, *Robin Hood,* when he adds "it is still possible that [the lines] were written by Shakespeare himself and form part of an earlier draft of the play"[10] but this and many of his other oft repeated assertions about Herne remain problematic.

What Matthew's work on Herne highlights is a common issue with presentations of Herne in the twenty-first century – that precedence is confidently claimed for various traditions with a confusing sense of where they came from. The resurgence of interest in folklore in recent years has seen this issue intensify. For example, in *Woodland Folktales of Britain and Ireland,* Lisa Schneidau states that the figure of Herne "drinks from a much deeper well of folklore [before *Merry Wives*]. Many people have connected Herne to the Green Man, the shadowy British vegetation god, and Cernunnos, the Celtic horned god of the woodland. Others have pointed out that he may be a manifestation of the Woodwose, the wild man of the woods."[11]

She then goes on to recount a version of the story which is partially drawn from Ainsworth's *Windsor Castle* and partially from Halliwell-Phillipp's historical research into Rychard Horne, although neither of these two sources are credited. We see this time and again with Herne, where literary sources and individual research is presented as collective folklore.

However, while there are some issues with Schneidau's account, it is also a good illustration of another trend among the various accounts of Herne's tale in the twenty-first century; that we are continuing to build a new mythology around him. Schneidau's version of Herne's tale concludes with an anecdote, initially told by Ruth Tongue in 1964, about three young men, "Teddy boys,"[12] who were destroying an area of woodland in Windsor when they found a silver horn. When they blew it, the Wild Hunt pursued them to a local church. Two of them made it inside safely while the third "fell quite dead on the steep with an invisible arrow right through him."[13]

Picking which of the many new stories about Herne will go on to have the most significant impact on his folklore is difficult, but there are some striking re-imaginings that have appeared so far this century. Perhaps the most beautiful and unsettling is in Patrick Ness's 2011 novel for young adults, *A Monster Calls.* It tells the story of Conor O'Malley, a boy who is trying to deal with the consequences of his mother's illness and impending death. Connor finds himself waking up from the same dream at the same time each night. Looking out of his window, he sees "the great yew tree that rose from the centre of the graveyard, a tree so ancient it almost seemed to be made of the same stone as the church."[14] However, the tree does not stay in the churchyard for very long:

> As Conor watched the uppermost branches of the tree gathered themselves into a great and terrible face, shimmering into a mouth and nose and even eyes, peering back at him. Other branches twisted around one another, always creaking, always groaning, until they formed two long arms and a second leg to set down beside the main trunk. The rest of the tree gathered itself into a spine and then a torso, the thin, needle-like leaves weaving together to make a green, furry skin that moved and breathed as if there were muscles and lungs underneath.[15]

On a separate visit, Conor asks the monster who they are:

> *I have as many names as there are years to time itself!* roared the monster. *I am Herne the Hunter! I am Cernunnos! I am the eternal Green Man! ...I am the spine that the mountains hang upon! I am the tears the rivers cry! I am the lungs that breathe the wind! I am the wolf that kills the stag, the hawk that kills the mouse, the spider that kills the fly! I am the stag, the mouse and the fly that are eaten! I am the snake of the world devouring its tail! I am everything untamed and untameable!* It brought Conor up close to its eye. *I am this wild earth, come for you Conor O'Malley.*[16]

While this version of Herne may seem completely unique, it does share common traits with previous incarnations. Just like Susan Cooper's interpretation, Ness's Herne is an elemental force, although it is rooted in the plant rather than the animal realm, as is the case in *The Dark is Rising*. This version of Herne also has much in common with the character in *The Box of Delights*. Just as Masefield's Herne helps Kay to see clearly, Ness' Monster tells Conor a series of stories which force him to confront his increasingly difficult and destructive emotions.

Another beautiful vision of Herne is conjured by Nick Hayes in *The Book of Trespass*. Hayes, as it turns out, is the 'Nick' interviewed by Grayson Perry in *Full English*, the programme which started this journey for me back in 2023. In *The Book of Trespass*, Hayes takes a series of journeys around England to consider the implications of private land ownership on the English psyche and our right to roam. The final chapter sees Hayes in Windsor, where he is "looking for a place to set up camp, to spend the day and its night in an open-eyed vigil for Herne."[17] He begins by recounting what he considers to be the authentic folklore surrounding Herne, which is, essentially, the story invented by Ainsworth, of Richard II's skilled hunter being magically saved after a close shave with death. As with Schneidau, Hayes does not credit this story to Ainsworth. It is also interesting to remember that the character of Herne intervenes in Ainsworth's novel to tell us that the story is not true.

Hayes wonders if he can get to see the replanted Herne's Oak, which had "resisted the cult of exclusion right up to 1848."[18] These days, however, Herne's Oak is firmly off limits, with Hayes noting that "a single foot on this turf will land me in jail for a year, with an unlimited fine."[19]

While weighing up his options, Hayes muses on Herne himself, recounting the story that Herne predates Shakespeare and is connected to ancient horned gods and the figure of the Green Man, before he starts to weave a very different figure: "And though there is no documented evidence of this, the legend of Herne seems to have influenced the spirit of sedition in Berkshire"[20] he claims. The key to Herne's potency is his story: "In short, Herne is wild, untameable, terrifying inspiring and seriously cool; he is literally a legend. I want to see the tree. I want to touch it, to connect to this long thread of storytelling that worships the unruliness of the wild wood over the order of the mown lawn."[21]

"These stories are spells"[22] Hayes continues, before conjuring a vision of Herne which will last long in the memory:

> If England really wants to take back control, it should take it from the anachronistic system of ownership that has left so many of its people dispossessed of their rights. Herne leads the immigrants, the Diaspora, the hippies, the fracking protestors, the small farmers who commit suicide at the rate of one a week, the ramblers, the entire rental market, the ravers, anyone in England who is ostracised by their lack of access to the value of the land. But in the Herne legend at least, they have horses, they have power and they have finally risen – change is on the way.[23]

Hayes' emphatic evocation of Herne's allyship is incredibly empowering. It is a vision of Herne positioned as the champion of the underdog, something which absolutely chimes with the English sense of national character.

Zoe Gilbert's 2022 novel *The Mischief Acts* takes Hayes' idea of the potency of Herne's story and translates it into an expansive and compelling narrative which is sure to enchant generations of Herne's followers. What will be even more interesting is to see which elements of Gilbert's narrative become established parts of Herne's folklore over the next few years! It is likely to be the most influential text written on Herne so far in the twenty-first century. It is certainly the most lyrical and thought-provoking.

When asked to define Herne the Hunter, Gilbert writes:

> He's as much an anti-hero as a hero, I think. Herne the Hunter is one of those characters in British folklore who has no clear origin story, and he has been many things to many people. The accepted stories around him that you can easily find on the internet now, presented as traditional lore, actually derive from other fiction: Shakespeare, for example, or a version of the creation of Herne invented by a 19th century novelist. Essentially Herne is a sort of 'horned god' archetype, with connections to figures like Cernunnos, the Celtic horned god of the forest, and Odin, as a leader of the wild hunt – galloping through stormy skies and collecting the souls of the dead. He has antlers, he belongs in the forest, he loves to hunt, he is scary and powerful. But he is also connected through lore to tricksters and entertainers like Puck, Robin Goodfellow, Pan, and Harlequin. This huge web of connection coalesced in my version of Herne, who fancies himself as a subversive mischief-maker, but is also dangerous when threatened. Because of his attachment to the wood – he is a kind of genius loci of the forest, and cannot exist without it – when the wood comes under threat, Herne does too. So, in Mischief Acts, Herne represents the defence of a wild place, but he also represents our own inner wildness and need for mischief. He's the transgressive force in all of us that can get out of control when the pressure is on.[24]

The novel "weaves the story of the Great North Wood – the forest that once stretched across today's south London – with the legend of Herne the Hunter, a horned spirit purported to roam the wood."[25] Again, Herne is dislocated from Windsor but, this time, not as far as Nottinghamshire. Gilbert's novel is presented in three sections, titled *Enchantment, Dis-Enchantment* and *Re-Enchantment*, charting the progress of how reason affects humanity's relationship with Herne and the wider natural world. Living close and within the Great North Wood, the characters in the early chapters live cheek-by-jowl with a cast of fantastical characters. The age of reason forms the core of *Dis-Enchantment*, as Herne's influence slowly drains away and the wood is cut down in the name of progress. *Re-Enchantment* takes the reader into a somewhat dystopian future, as mankind again finds themselves engaging with the woodland because of climate change. Each chapter can stand alone, although there are motifs and echoes which work throughout the text, which increase in potency the more you read it. For example, the character of Bearman appears in the first chapter and brings Herne back from the dead, while versions of him appear with slight name variations as the novel progresses.

Gilbert begins the story in 1392 with the chapter *Herne the Hunter*, which is, broadly, a retelling of the tale created by Ainsworth, but vividly wrought in beautiful language:

> As if in a nightmare, Herne stood.
> He filled the wood with a kind of glamour,
> Made his own Moon, to light that demon crown of his,
> To light the length of rope that trailed still from his neck
> ...
> Herne, the king's angel of the hunt, now demon.
> Herne, Antlered, magicked from the Great Oak,
> Dead and risen, dead and risen once more.[26]

Chapter 2 moves the story forward to 1451 where Bearman's daughter, Agnes, confides that she loved Herne and that Bearman attached horns to Herne's head because he "found out, that I loved Herne. He couldn't stand it. He said Herne was wayward and foxy and rascally wild, and he was right. That's why I loved him."[27] Chapter 3, moves to 1500 and another love story, this time between Herne and the Naiad, Effra. This love is deep and passionate, with Herne's phrase "My pleasure is in the Hunt"[28] alternating between an excuse for gaslighting the naiad and being deeply sexual. Chapter 4 takes place in 1606 and is called *The Lord of Misrule*. One of my favourite chapters of the novel, Herne becomes the Master of the Revels for Edward Alleyn, a retired stage actor. Alleyn was a contemporary of Shakespeare, known to have acted in several of his plays, although Shakespeare is neatly omitted from this tale. Alleyn and his fellow revellers prepare a staging of the play *Herne the Hunter* under the guidance of one M. Herne, which descends into abject chaos with the conjuring of the real Wild Hunt. Chapter 5 shifts to 1691 and the tale of "A woman highwayman, with horns. In a red gown. With bow and arrows, to boot"[29] called Oberon.

As the reader moves into the time of *Dis-Enchantment*, the action moves to 1760 and the tale of *The Erl-King's Daughter*. Based on the historical figure of the notoriously scandalous actress Ann Catley, Gilbert makes her Herne's descendant. Chapter 7, set in 1797, reflects on the process of enclosure, with Herne reduced to being a de-horned gardener, while Chapter 8, set in 1821, sees the symbolic killing of a heron by a hawk, as Herne muses that "if the wood is chopped up, shared out, reduced to crumbs, so will he be."[30] Chapter 9 moves forward to 1877 and sees Mr Ship wanting to cut down some trees in the shadow of Crystal Palace to build a scientific school in memory of his friend. However, Mr Ship's plans are thwarted when he finds a group of "little people"[31] dressed in different theatrical costumes, including the Harlequin, around the trees he wants to destroy. By 1936, Herne has become a dreamy bad-boy who is responsible for setting fire to the Crystal Palace while, in Chapter 11, the naiad Effra reemerges into the drug-fuelled haze of the 1960s. The final two chapters of *Dis-Enchantment* are astonishing. *Hurlecane,* set in 1987, sees Herne conjure the great storm which notoriously caused so much disruption across southern England in that year:

> Herne summons his voice from the earth. Drunk on fury, close to death, Herne will not be forgotten. This time he will take what has been taken, wreck what has been wrecked. He wants more than fire.
> Herne summons the sky.
> His aim is careless.[32]

Chapter 13 tells the story of Kate and Richard. Kate is (perhaps jokingly) planning on sleeping with the gardener, the handsome and tanned Tom. Richard storms out in horror, stomping through the only tiny fragment of the Great North Wood that remains to the pub, The Green Man. However, he is struck and killed by the branch of a tree. As he slowly decomposes in the forest, his family search desperately for him.

The final section, *Re-Enchantment,* is more cohesive than the previous sections, telling the story of how humanity reengages with the woodland as a place of sanctuary during the heat of summers influenced by climate change. The woods are reclaimed and restored, and so Herne comes back, as the wolf-raised character, Herndon, in the final chapter, but, perhaps more magically as a flock of starlings in Chapter 15:

> And then it got properly weird. Because the starlings, they'd started making these shapes in the sky, like living clouds, like tornadoes, all sorts.
>
> The one evening, right above the north boundary of the forest, they flew up and made the shape of a stag's head.
>
> Only lasted a few seconds.

> But hundreds of people saw it, right up there near the city. Some woman filmed it.[33]

The novel is bookended by academic writing, as if it were framing a collection of evidence exploring the existence of Herne over time. In a transcript of a fictional lecture at the end of the book, the character of D. Ferrero reflects on the picture of the starling murmuration and the human compulsion to spot patterns and make connections:

> This photograph was taken in South London in 2058. What do you see? Come on, it's not hard, is it? Yes, to our human eyes, there's the very obvious shape of a stag's head. The starlings won't see it that way, but we do. We can't help ourselves ... Once you know the murmuration is made up of individual starlings, it doesn't fall apart or disappear. In fact, it's more marvellous than ever.[34]

In other words, Herne is not made up of one single perspective, of one single part of his folklore. He is the sum of all our perspectives, of all the disparate beliefs we have explored about him throughout this book, swirling together.

And that is the great achievement of Gilbert's book with its trickster Herne, who at once terrifies, repulses, scares and entices us. Gilbert weaves her new folklore around existing tales, tying Herne's kaleidoscopic persona to the changing way we perceive our world. While we may not like every vision she conjures, somewhere among the tales we will find one that resonates with us. That does not make the others any less valid, but rather teaches us to embrace Herne in all his diversity.

Conclusion

Our Herne

It would have been an enormous stroke of luck for Shakespeare to have found a horned spirit haunting a tree in Windsor when he needed a joke about horns for the final scene of *The Merry Wives of Windsor*. The chances of him finding a story which would fit exactly are incredibly remote.

It does seem, though, that he found something. The fact the play references a specific tree, a local landmark, does suggest that Shakespeare may not have completely made Herne up. After all, "The allusion would lose all its effect if there had not been a real Herne's Oak, and a real ghost story to go with it."[1]

But what if Shakespeare did find a story set around a local tree and changed it to fit his play? We know that Shakespeare was not a folklorist. He was a playwright and so the stories he told had to develop the dramatic action of his plays, not necessarily be true to an original tale. What if Shakespeare got confused, or deliberately changed the tale of Herne? What if, in the original folklore, it was the tree that was meant to have the horns and not the ghost? After all we have testimony from a Windsor local, Charles Knight, which suggests this. His testimony has been dismissed for centuries but what if there is a grain of truth there? Eric L. Fitch notes that "The oak probably ended up stag-headed, which means that it had dead branches at its top sticking up above the green-leaved branches, looking rather like the antlers of a stag."[2] Those eighteenth-century etchings of Herne's Oak could, possibly, show a tree with horns.

Is that theory as farfetched as the proposition that Herne leads the Wild Hunt, when all the earliest records tell of a singular ghost bound to a tree and not one roaming the countryside? Or that he is an incarnation of Cernunnos or Woden, when his horns meant something very different to the audience at the time the folklore was first written down? And what if Herne, or Horne, were a real, historical person and the story that survived around the oak was a memory of, for example, Rychard Horne, after he was punished by Henry VIII?

While a figure with horns could be a horned god, it does not always have to be. Someone being hung on a tree does not always have to be Woden. Have we been so quick to bundle his story up with other pieces of lore that we have failed to see what is right in front of us?

In much the same way that people have questioned Shakespeare's authorship because they have created links between his works and those of his contemporaries, we have done the same with Herne. His folklore before Shakespeare is uncertain but because he is called 'the Hunter' and appeared on stage wearing horns, we have connected him with tropes such as the Wild Hunt and to a pantheon of horned gods.

In both cases, it took a while for those connections to be formed; it took until the nineteenth century for Shakespeare's authorship to be questioned and it was around the same time that Jacob Grimm first wrote that Herne was a god. As citizens of the twenty-first century, we often willingly accept the later analysis of a situation, believing that it must be more sophisticated than knowledge from earlier times. We like solving puzzles, we like making connections, even when those connections are not as secure as they may, at first, appear.

To really get to know Herne, we need to put aside our current interconnected view of him and go back to the beginning of his story, back to what our ancestors thought.

As Harte wrote back in 1996:

> Somewhere near the Castle, at any rate, an old oak tree stood in 1597: and Windsor people thought that it was haunted by a dead forester, who appeared in a form

> half-man, half-stag. That seems a very slender edifice foundation on which to raise the edifice of speculation which now celebrates Herne the Hunter. [3]

Have we seen the figure of a horned god when, if fact, it is a murmuration of starlings?

I have asked some difficult questions in this book – did Shakespeare invent Herne? What if the horns were meant to be on the tree? What if Herne's position as a leader of the Wild Hunt, as an echo of Cernunnos, Woden and a form of the Green Man, is not as secure as we believed? I have also highlighted concerns about the work of influential writers such as Jacob Grimm, Margaret Murray, T. Lowe Thompson, and John Matthews. The reason I have done both of those things is that I believe looking for a single, ancient lineage for Herne is deeply problematic. Claims that he is linked to Woden or Cernunnos can never be substantiated. There simply are not the documents to join all the dots.

Do we need solid evidence? In her book on the goddess, Danu Forest reflects on the fact that some scholars assert that Cerridwen was never worshipped as divine. "However," Forest proposes, "with other eyes it is possible and credible to see the traces of far earlier spiritual practices in the bardic tradition, which over the course of time survived and perhaps diminished in the Christian period from what was once an ecstatic, visionary cult…"[4]

Can the same be said of Herne? Many people believe so, although they do differ on which ancient deity he sprang from.

If you do have a singular view of Herne's character and lineage, then I hope I have been able to introduce a little bit of doubt into your mind because Herne may not be what you think he is. I say that because he cannot be everything that we say he is.[5] He cannot be both the ghost of Rychard Horne and the ancient leader of the Wild Hunt. He certainly is not a demon and probably does not date as far back as the reign of Richard II, despite a growing number of books telling us he does.

Not every belief about Herne can be right – but why do some of us have to be wrong? I do not believe that there should be one dogmatic way of seeing Herne, because there has never been one way of seeing him. He is what every century has made him. His diversity is his greatest strength. Exploring his many faces while writing this book has made me love Herne more, not less.

Do I think he is an ancient Lord of the Forest? Well, that is not important, is it? It is not what I think that matters. It is what we think, together, that is important. Herne's position among the pantheon of neo-pagan gods is secure for one simple reason: he is the Lord of the Forest because that is what we need him to be. We have created 'Good Old Herne' because there is no one else in England quite like him.

We have witnessed him change from a human, hanged for a crime or out of shame, whose ghost haunts a tree, to a spirit which inhabits a tree, to a spirit which inhabits England's woodland, to a deity who physically and emotionally embodies our forests. We hold that lineage, with all its contradictions, because Herne speaks to a deep need in the English psyche, for ghost stories, for a sense of connection to the landscape, for a magical edge to our everyday lives.

At a time when we have found ourselves disconnected from nature, Herne has become a key symbol for the potency of our woodlands and our relationship with them. Whether he is an ancient god or one we have created together, that does not stop him from being exactly what we need right now.

Gilbert is right, exploring the history of Herne the Hunter is like looking at a murmuration of starlings, with them twisting and turning to create new and different shapes. Herne lies not in the individual starlings but in the gaps between them, in the twists and turns which make and reshape them into new forms. In two hundred years' time, Herne will be very different to how we see him today. He will slip from our grasp and belong to others.

Herne is not just Shakespeare's Device, Ireland's Ghost, Ainsworth's Demon, Carpenter's Shaman, or Gilbert's Starlings. He is all of them. And none of them.

He is our Herne.

Endnotes

Introduction – Who Is Herne?

1. Ryan and Matthews (2024) p151
2. Patterson (2023) p56
3. Hutton (2014) p382

Chapter 1 – Shakespeare's Device

1. This and all other quotations from the play are taken from the Oxford single edition of the play, edited by T.W. Craik (1990)
2. Shapiro (2010) p10
3. Shapiro (2010) p17
4. Shapiro (2010) p3
5. Shapiro (2010) p313
6. http://www.shakespearesway.org/ (accessed 13/09/2024)
7. Salingar (2001) p10
8. Melchiori (2000) p257
9. Craik (1990) p193
10. Harte (1996) p32
11. Harte (1996) p28
12. Hutton (2014) p391-392
13. https://www.britannica.com/topic/witching-hour (accessed 25/11/2024)
14. Craik (1990) p204, n.5
15. Pliny the Younger, quoted in https://hypnogoria.com/folklore_chainedghosts.html (accessed 25/11/2024)
16. Salingar (2001) p10
17. https://www.etymonline.com/word/cuckold (accessed 10/01/2025)
18. Wells and Taylor (1997) p341

19. Melchiori (2000) pm257,n.26
20. https://www.oed.com/dictionary/keeper_n?tab=meaning_and_use#40083489 (accessed 16/02/2025)
21. https://www.oed.com/dictionary/woodman_n1?tab=meaning_and_use#14286792 (accessed 16/02/2025)
22. Marlowe, https://www.gutenberg.org/files/779/779-h/779-h.htm (accessed 10/01/2025)
23. Harte (1996) p28
24. Harte (1996) p30
25. Davies (2007) p52-53
26. Davies (2024) p25
27. Salingar (2001) p9-10

Chapter 2 – Ireland's Ghost

1. Harte (1996) p28
2. https://windsorlocalhistorygroup.org/putting-windsor-on-the-map/ (accessed 17/01/2025)
3. Taylor (1990) p10
4. Taylor (1990) p13
5. Davies (2024) p38
6. https://www.rct.uk/collection/917551/hernes-oak (accessed 17/01/2025)
7. https://www.rct.uk/collection/search#/14/collection/700763/hernes-oak-windsor-little-park-1777 (accessed 17/01//2025)
8. https://www.rct.uk/collection/search#/1/collection/700757/hernes-oak (accessed 17/01/2025)
9. Harte (1996) p28
10. https://www.shakespeare.org.uk/explore-shakespeare/shakespedia/david-garrick-jubilee/ (accessed 17/01/2025)
11. Pierce (2004) p22
12. Pierce (2004) pxiii
13. Pierce (2004) p41
14. Ireland (1792) p15-16

15. Ireland (1792) p16-17
16. Ireland (1792) p17
17. Ireland (1792) p18
18. Ireland (1792) p19
19. Stoughton (1844) p156-157
20. Wright (1796)
21. Ireland (1792) p16

Chapter 3 – Ainsworth's Demon

1. https://www.treeterms.co.uk/files/definitions/maiden-forestry-.html (accessed 14/02/2025)
2. Perry (1867) p7
3. Perry (1867) p4
4. Perry (1867) p7-8
5. Perry (1867) p58
6. windsormuseum.org.uk/collection/bust-of-william-shakespeare-carved-from-a-portion-of-hernes-oak-by-w-perry-1864/ (accessed 14/02/2025)
7. Perry (1867) p43
8. Roberts (1997) p99
9. Perry (1867) p1
10. Perry (1867) p57
11. Perry (1867) p58
12. Perry (1867) p57
13. Ireland (1792) p16
14. Halliwell-Phillipps (1842) pxxxi-pxxxii
15. Perry (1867) p5
16. Perry (1867) p4 n
17. Halliwell-Phillipps (1842) pxxxii
18. Perry (1867) p4
19. Perry (1867) p12
20. Perry (1867) p7
21. Perry (1867) p12
22. Perry (1867) p53

23. https://www.tapatalk.com/groups/theroyalwindsorforum/herne-the-hunter-herne-s-oak-t777.html (accessed 15/02/2025)
24. https://windsorlocalhistorygroup.org/hernes-oak/ (accessed 15/02/2025)
25. Grimm, (1883) p918
26. Forest (2018) p67-68
27. Grimm (1883) p942
28. Grimm (1883) p942 n.
29. Hutton (2014) p1
30. Hutton (2014) p3-4
31. Carver (2020) pxiii
32. Carver (2020) p63
33. Carver (2020) p120-121
34. Ainsworth (n.d.) p15
35. Ainsworth (n.d.) p 18
36. Ainsworth (n.d.) p20
37. Ainsworth (n.d) p278
38. Ainsworth (n.d) p222
39. Ainsworth (n.d) p132
40. Ainsworth (n.d) p95
41. Ainsworth (n.d) p145-146
42. Ainsworth (n.d) p135
43. Ainsworth (n.d) p278
44. Ainsworth (n.d) p311
45. Ainsworth (n.d) p154
46. Ainsworth (n.d) p325
47. Ainsworth (n.d) p222
48. Ainsworth (n.d) p376
49. Ainsworth (n.d) p382
50. Ainsworth (n.d) p109
51. Ainsworth (n.d) p97
52. Ainsworth (n.d) p131
53. Ainsworth (n.d) p135

54. Ainsworth (n.d) p59-60
55. Ainsworth (n.d) p133
56. Ainsworth (n.d) p146
57. Carver (2020) p150
58. Ainsworth (n.d) p68
59. Ainsworth (n.d) p111
60. Ainsworth (n.d) p132
61. Ainsworth (n.d) p140
62. Ainsworth (n.d) p39-40
63. Ainsworth (n.d) p40
64. Harte (1996) p30-31
65. Ainsworth (n.d) p145
66. St Michael (2008) p35
67. Ainsworth (n.d) p241
68. Ainsworth (n.d) p241
69. Ainsworth (n.d) p241
70. Ainsworth (n.d) p243
71. Ainsworth (n.d) p244
72. Ainsworth (n.d) p244
73. Ainsworth (n.d) p245
74. Ainsworth (n.d) p245
75. Ainsworth (n.d) p246
76. Ainsworth (n.d) p247
77. Ainsworth (n.d) p247
78. Ainsworth (n.d) p247
79. Ainsworth (n.d) p247
80. Ainsworth (n.d) p249
81. Ainsworth (n.d) p250
82. Ainsworth (n.d) p250
83. Ainsworth (n.d) p251
84. Ainsworth (n.d) p252
85. Ainsworth (n.d) p252
86. Ainsworth (n.d) p319
87. Ainsworth (n.d) p313

88. Ainsworth (n.d) p318
89. Carver (2020) p149
90. Carver (2020) p150
91. Harte (1996) p31
92. Carver (2020) p213
93. Ainsworth (n.d) p146
94. Harte (1996) p31

Chapter 4 – Carpenter's Shaman

1. Macfarlane (2022) https://www.theguardian.com/books/2022/dec/03/midwinter-magic-robert-macfarlane-world-service-the-dark-is-rising-susan-cooper-bbc (accessed 07/03/2025)
2. Cooper (2013) p332
3. Cooper (2013) p 343
4. Cooper (2013) p339
5. Copper (2013) p339
6. Davies (2007) p4
7. Davies (2007) p228
8. Cooper (2013) p197
9. Cooper (2013) p194
10. Copper (2013) p194
11. Cooper (2013) p196-197
12. Cooper (2013) p333-334
13. Cooper (2013) p 337
14. Cooper (2013) p337
15. Cooper (2013) p338-339
16. Thompson (1929) p1
17. Thompson (1929) frontispiece
18. Thompson (1929) p55
19. Thompson (1929) p124
20. Thompson (1929) p125
21. Thompson (1929) p131-132
22. Thompson (1929) p133

23. Thompson (1929) p134
24. Thompson (1929) p134
25. Murray (1970) p11
26. Murray (1970) p33-34
27. Murray (1970) p34
28. Harte (1996) p32
29. Milner (2024) p39
30. Harte (1996) p32
31. Savage (2022) p121
32. Nichols (2002) p87
33. Masefield https://www.gutenberg.org/files/32532/32532-h/32532-h.htm (accessed 08/05/2025)
34. Ashe (2023) p160
35. Masefield (2008) p18
36. Masefield (2008) p29-30
37. There is a village called Condicote in the Cotswolds, close to where Masefield lived for a while, but there is no suggestion that his fictional county of Tatshire is, in fact, Gloucestershire.
38. Masefield (2008) p104
39. Masefield (2008) p104-105
40. Masefield (2008) p105
41. Masefield (2008) p106
42. Masefield (2008) p106
43. Masefield (2008) p108
44. Masefield (2008) p109
45. Masefield (2008) p256
46. Masefield (2008) p285
47. Masefield (2008) p286
48. Masefield (2008) p373
49. Masefield (2008) p375
50. Masefield (2008) p377
51. https://artandtheology.org/tag/john-masefield/ (accessed 14/03/2025)

52. Errington (2024) p66
53. Masefield (2008) p365
54. Torday (2017) p54
55. Torday (2017) p98
56. Torday (2017) p98
57. Torday (2023) p36
58. Kirkley (1992) p20-22
59. Power (1994) p24
60. Power (1994) p24
61. Harte (1996) p31
62. Harte (1996) p32

Chapter 5 – Gilbert's Starlings

1. Ryan and Matthews (2024) p151
2. https://www.shakespeare.org.uk/explore-shakespeare/blogs/herne-hunter-may-day-figure-folklore/ (accessed 21/03/2025)
3. https://www.churchtimes.co.uk/articles/2022/21-october/books-arts/book-reviews/the-green-man-in-medieval-england-christian-shoots-from-pagan-roots-by-stephen-miller (accessed 21/03/2025)
4. Matthews (2001) p114
5. Matthews (2001) p115
6. Matthews (2001) p115
7. Matthews (2001) p116
8. Matthews (2001) p114
9. Matthews (2001) p115
10. Matthews (2016) p55
11. Schneidau (2020) p55
12. Schneidau (2020) p59
13. Schneidau (2020 p59
14. Ness (2011) p14
15. Ness (2011) p14-15
16. Ness (2011) p44

17. Hayes (2020) p347
18. Hayes (2020) p349
19. Hayes (2020) p354
20. Hayes (2020) p354
21. Hayes (2020) p354
22. Hayes (2020) p380
23. Hayes (2020) p383
24. https://zoegilbert.com/interview/ (accessed 21/03/2025)
25. Scheffer (2022) https://www.the-tls.co.uk/literature/fiction/mischief-acts-zoe-gilbert-book-review-pablo-scheffer (accessed 21/03/2025)
26. Gilbert (2022) p15-16
27. Gilbert (2022) p40
28. Gilbert (2022) p71
29. Gilbert (2022) p117
30. Gilbert (2022) p200
31. Gilbert (2022) p215
32. Gilbert (2022) p178
33. Gilbert (2022) p382
34. Gilbert (20022) p415-416

Conclusion – Our Herne

1. Harte (1996) p28
2. Fitch, Erik L. (2024) p54
3. Harte (1996) p29
4. Forest (2024) p6
5. A summary of the variations of Herne in "folk tales" can be found in Fitch (2024) p30-34

Bibliography

Ainsworth, William Harrison, *Windsor Castle,* Collins, London and Glasgow, n.d.

Ashe, Geoffrey, *Mythology of the British Isles*, Canelo, London, 2023.

Carver, Stephen, *The Author who Outsold Dickens*, Pen and Sword Books, Barnsley, 2020.

Chainey, Dee Dee and Winsham, Willow, *Treasury of Folklore: Woodlands and Forests*, B.T. Batsford, London, 2021.

Cooper, Susan, *The Dark is Rising*, Vintage, London, 2013.

Davies, Sioned (ed. and trans.), *The Mabinogion,* Oxford University Press, Oxford, 2007.

Elcock, Stephen and Osman, Mat, *England on Fire,* Watkins, London, 2022.

Errington, Philip W, *Opening The Box of Delights,* New Edition, Darton, Longman and Todd, Croydon, 2024.

Fitch Eric. L, *Herne the Hunter of Windsor Forest*, Green Magic, Street, 2024.

Forest, Danu, *Cerridwen*, Moon Books, Winchester, 2024.

Forest, Danu, *Gwyn Ap Nudd*, Moon Books, Winchester, 2018.

Freebury-Jones, Darren, *Shakespeare's Borrowed Feathers*, Manchester University Press, Manchester, 2024.

Gilbert, Zoe, *Mischief Acts*, Bloomsbury Circus, London, 2022.

Grimm, Jacob, *Teutonic Mythology,* Volume 3, translated James Steven Stallybrass, George Bell and Son, London, 1883, found at https://archive.org/details/jacob-grimm-teutonic-mythology-english-translation-volume-3_202208/page/n3/mode/2up (accessed 15/02/2025)

Halliwell-Phillipps, James Orchard, *The First Sketch of Shakespeare's Merry Wives of Windsor,* The Shakespeare Society, London, 1842, found at https://archive.org/details/firstsketchshak00hallgoog (accessed 15/02/2025)

Harte, Jeremy, *Herne the Hunter – A Case of Mistaken Identity*, in *At the Edge*, No 3, September 1996, pp27-33.

Hayes, Nick, The Book of Trespass, Bloomsbury, London, 2020.

Hutton, Ronald, *Pagan Britain*, Yale University Press, London, 2014.

Hutton, Ronald, *The Wild Hunt and the Witches' Sabbat*, University of Bristol, Bristol, 2014, available at: https://research-information.bris.ac.uk/ws/portalfiles/portal/38162196/WildHunt_first_edit.pdf

Ireland, Samuel, *Picturesque views on the river Thames, from its source in Glocestershire to the Nore; with observations on the public buildings and other works of art in its vicinity, volume 2*, T&L Egerton, Whitehall, London, 1792.

Jones, Kelvin, *The Green Man* in *Fantasy Tales*, Winter, 1983 pages 40-43.

Kirkley, Paul, *Robin of Sherwood*, in *TV Zone*, Issue 26, January 1992, found here https://www.robinofsherwood.org/articles/TV-Zone26_199201_RoS.pdf (accessed 15/03/2025).

Macfarlane, Robert, *Midwinter magic: Robert Macfarlane on the enduring power of The Dark is Rising*, in *The Guardian*, 3rd December 2022, available at: https://www.theguardian.com/books/2022/dec/03/midwinter-magic-robert-macfarlane-world-service-the-dark-is-rising-susan-cooper-bbc (accessed 07/03/2025).

Marlowe, Christopher, *The Tragical History of Doctor Faustus*, found at: https://www.gutenberg.org/files/779/779-h/779-h.htm (accessed 25/11/2024).

Masefield, John, *The Box of Delights*, Egmont, London, 2008.

Masefield, John, *King Cole*, found at: https://www.gutenberg.org/files/32532/32532-h/32532-h.htm (accessed 08/03/2025).

Matthews, John, *Robin Hood*, Amberley Publishing, London, 2016.

Matthews, John, *The Quest for the Green Man*, Godsfield Press, London, 2001.

McCrum, Robert, *Who Really Wrote Shakespeare*, in *The Guardian*, 14th March 2010.

Milner, Nicky, *Star Carr: Life after the ice*, York Publishing Services Ltd, York, 2024.

Milward, Emily, Herne the Hunter: a May Day Figure of Folklore, found at: https://www.shakespeare.org.uk/explore-shakespeare/blogs/herne-hunter-may-day-figure-folklore/ (accessed 21/03/2025).

Murray, Margaret, *The God of the Witches*, Oxford University Press, London, 1970.

Ness, Patrick, *A Monster Calls*, Walker Books, London, 2011.

Nichols, Ross, *Cole of the Chilterns* in *In the Grove of the Druids*, edited by Philip Carr-Gomm, Watkins Publishing, London, 2002.

Patterson, Rachael, *The Gods and Goddesses of England*, Moon Books, Winchester, 2023.

Perry, William, *A Treatise on the identity of Herne's Oak, shewing the Maiden Tree to have been the Real One*, London, L Booth, 1867 found at https://ia800909.us.archive.org/25/items/atreatiseoniden00perrgoog/atreatiseoniden00perrgoog.pdf (accessed 14/02/2025).

Pierce, Patricia, *The Great Shakespeare Fraud*, Sutton Publishing, Stroud, 2004.

Power, Ty, *Nothing is ever Forgotten*, in *Dreamwatch*, number 3, December 1994, found at: https://www.robinofsherwood.org/articles/DreamWatch3_199412_RoS.pdf (accessed 15/03/2025).

Roberts, Jane, Royal Landscape: The Gardens and Parks of Windsor, Yale University Press, 1997.

Ryan, Mark and John Matthews, *The Sherwood Oracle*, Sterling Ethos, New York, 2024

Salingar, Leo, *The Englishness of The Merry Wives of Windsor*, in *Cahiers Élisabéthains*, Volume 59, Issue 1, April 2001, pp9-25.

Savage, Mabh, *Cernunnos* in *Naming the God*, edited by Trevor Greenfield, Moon Books, Winchester, 2022.

Scheffer, Pablo, The return of Herne the Hunter, in the Times Literary Supplement, 1 April 2022, found at: https://www.the-tls.co.uk/literature/fiction/mischief-acts-zoe-gilbert-book-review-pablo-scheffer (accessed 21/03/2025).

Schneidau, Lisa, *Woodland Folk Tales of Britain and Ireland,* The History Press, Cheltenham, 2020.

Shakespeare, William, *The Merry Wives of Windsor*, ed T.W. Craik, Oxford World Shakespeare, Oxford University Press, Oxford, 1990.

Shakespeare, William, The Merry Wives of Windsor, ed Sarah Neville with an introduction by Callan Davies, Oxford World's Classics, Oxford University Press, Oxford, 2024.

Shakespeare, William, *The Merry Wives of Windsor*, ed Giorgio Melchiori, Arden Shakespeare Third series, Bloomsbury Publishing, 2000.

Shakespeare, William, *The Merry Wives of Windsor*, ed H.J. Oliver, Arden Shakespeare Second series, Methuen, London, 1971.

Shapiro, James, *Contested Will: Who Wrote Shakespeare?* Faber and Faber, London, 2010.

St Michael, Hortus, *Herne: The Royal Hunter* in *Horns of Power*, edited by Sorita d'Este, Avalonia, London, 2008.

Stoughton, John, *Noticed of Windsor in the Olden Time*, David Bogue, London, 1844, from https://laudatortemporisacti.blogspot.com/2011/11/felling-of-hernes-oak.html (accessed 14/02/2025).

Taylor, Gary, *Reinventing Shakespeare*, Vintage, London, 1990.

Thompson, R Lowe, *The History of the Devil: The Horned God of the West*, Keegan Paul, Trench, Trubner & co, London, 1929.

Torday, Piers, *The Box of Delights*, Wilton Music Hall edition, Faber and Faber, London, 2017.

Torday, Piers, *The Box of Delights,* RSC edition, Faber and Faber, London, 2023.

Wells, Stanley and Taylor, Gary, *William Shakespeare: A Textual Companion*, W.W. Norton and Company, New York, London, 1997.

Wright, Thomas, *Upon Herne's Oak being cut down, in the spring of 1796,* from https://laudatortemporisacti.blogspot.com/2011/11/felling-of-hernes-oak.html (accessed 17/01/2025).

Media Resources

The Box of Delights, 40th Anniversary Edition, Dir. Renny Rye, BBC, 2024, DVD.

Grayson Perry's Full English, Channel 4, 2023, available on Channel 4 streaming service.

Robin of Sherwood, The Complete Series, Network, 1983-86, DVD.

Online Resources

Art and Theology: https://artandtheology.org (accessed 14/03/2025).

Britannica: https://www.britannica.com (accessed 25/11/2024).

British Folklore: https://britishfolklore.com/windsor-great-park/ (accessed 08/03/2025).

The Church Times: https://www.churchtimes.co.uk (accessed 21/03/2025).

Etymology Online: https://www.etymonline.com (accessed 10/1/2025).

The Oxford English Dictionary: https://www.oed.com/ (accessed 23/02/2025).

Project Guttenberg: https://www.gutenberg.org (accessed 10/01/2025).

The Royal Collection Trust: https://www.rct.uk (accessed 17/01/2025).

The Shakespeare Birthplace Trust: https://www.shakespeare.org.uk (accessed 17/01/2025).

The Shakespeare Blog: https://theshakespeareblog.com/ (accessed 14/02/2025).

Shakespeare's Way: http://www.shakespearesway.org/ (accessed 13/09/2024).
Spirit of Sherwood: https://www.robinofsherwood.org/ (accessed 15/03/2025).
Tapatalk: https://www.tapatalk.com/) accessed 15/02/2025).
Tree Terms: https://www.treeterms.co.uk (accessed 14/02/2025).
Windsor Local History Group: https://windsorlocalhistorygroup.org (accessed 17/01/2025).
Zoe Gilbert: https://zoegilbert.com

MOON BOOKS

PAGANISM & SHAMANISM

What is Paganism? A religion, a spirituality, an alternative belief system, nature worship? You can find support for all these definitions (and many more) in dictionaries, encyclopaedias, and text books of religion, but subscribe to any one and the truth will evade you. Above all Paganism is a creative pursuit, an encounter with reality, an exploration of meaning and an expression of the soul. Druids, Heathens, Wiccans and others, all contribute their insights and literary riches to the Pagan tradition. Moon Books invites you to begin or to deepen your own encounter, right here, right now.

If you have enjoyed this book, why not tell other readers by posting a review on your preferred book site.

Bestsellers from Moon Books

Keeping Her Keys

An Introduction to Hekate's Modern Witchcraft

Cyndi Brannen

Blending Hekate, witchcraft and personal development together to create a powerful new magickal perspective.

Paperback: 978-1-78904-075-3 ebook 978-1-78904-076-0

Journey to the Dark Goddess

How to Return to Your Soul

Jane Meredith

Discover the powerful secrets of the Dark Goddess and transform your depression, grief and pain into healing and integration.

Paperback: 978-1-84694-677-6 ebook: 978-1-78099-223-5

Shamanic Reiki

Expanded Ways of Working with Universal Life Force Energy

Llyn Roberts, Robert Levy

Shamanism and Reiki are each powerful ways of healing; together, their power multiplies. Shamanic Reiki introduces techniques to help healers and Reiki practitioners tap ancient healing wisdom.

Paperback: 978-1-84694-037-8 ebook: 978-1-84694-650-9

Southern Cunning

Folkloric Witchcraft in the American South

Aaron Oberon

Modern witchcraft with a Southern flair, this book is a journey through the folklore of the American South and a look at the power these stories hold for modern witches.

Paperback: 978-1-78904-196-5 ebook: 978-1-78904-197-2

Bestsellers from Moon Books
Pagan Portals Series

The Morrigan
Meeting the Great Queens
Morgan Daimler
Ancient and enigmatic, the Morrigan reaches out to us. On shadowed wings and in raven's call, meet the ancient Irish goddess of war, battle, prophecy, death, sovereignty, and magic.
Paperback: 978-1-78279-833-0 ebook: 978-1-78279-834-7

The Awen Alone
Walking the Path of the Solitary Druid
Joanna van der Hoeven
An introductory guide for the solitary Druid, The Awen Alone will accompany you as you explore, and seek out your own place within the natural world.
Paperback: 978-1-78279-547-6 ebook: 978-1-78279-546-9

Moon Magic
Rachel Patterson
An introduction to working with the phases of the Moon, what they are and how to live in harmony with the lunar year and to utilise all the magical powers it provides.
Paperback: 978-1-78279-281-9 ebook: 978-1-78279-282-6

Hekate
A Devotional
Vivienne Moss
Hekate, Queen of Witches and the Shadow-Lands, haunts the pages of this devotional bringing magic and enchantment into your lives.
Paperback: 978-1-78535-161-7 ebook: 978-1-78535-162-4